D0617162

# PRAISE FOR *DIGITAL BUSINESS TRANSFORMATION*

"Written during the most extraordinary time in living memory, Nigel has created a timely playbook for leaders to accelerate transformation journeys through the post-pandemic rebound and towards renewed growth. This book outlines *why* and *how* businesses should constantly disrupt themselves and create new working models that will support shifting the organizational mindset. At a time when inclusivity, sustainability and trust in business is more needed than ever, *Digital Business Transformation* captures the multi-faceted nature of building a better future during this great reset for businesses, customers and society."

**—Alain Bejjani, CEO, Majid Al Futtaim**

"Successful approaches to ongoing transformation and evolution require a big picture, socio-technical approach. Nigel distills his lifetime of experience in working with top leaders and organizations into *Digital Business Transformation*, which masterfully sets out the connected capabilities and culture shifts necessary for any modern enterprise to create ongoing value for their customers and business."

**—Anthony Mullen, Senior Research Director, Gartner**

"With consumer and business change accelerating faster than ever after the global pandemic of 2020, Nigel Vaz has crafted a compelling vision for technology-enabled business transformation in the post-COVID world. *Digital Business Transformation* powerfully charts the course for continuous, value-creating innovation by taking a rigorous and holistic enterprise-wide approach to transforming not just technology, but culture too."

**—Douglas Hayward, Research Director,**
**Worldwide Digital Strategy Services, IDC**

"Nigel shares practical tips on building a digital moat for traditional companies that are confronted with disruptive digital transformation. From the perspective of the automotive industry that is navigating change across the car as an IOT platform, electrification and automation, *Digital Business Transformation* pulls together many pragmatic frameworks to provide a playbook that addresses technological, consumer and societal change in perfect balance."

**—Mamatha Chamarthi, Chief Information Officer NA & APAC,**
**Fiat Chrysler Automobiles**

"Nigel's deep understanding of how businesses and markets are disrupted through the power of data and technology is balanced perfectly with his experience of the human elements of change. *Digital Business Transformation* is an exposition on why and how to abandon traditional linear strategies and think about transformation as a journey to delight customers as you ride the waves of change."

**—Mark McClennon, Global Chief Information Officer, Burberry**

"At T-Mobile, we thrive on the type of permanent disruption that Nigel Vaz artfully explores in *Digital Business Transformation*. This book is a great read for leaders who are focused on staying a step ahead of their customers' needs, wants and expectations. Nigel gives smart insight about the things we at the Un-carrier are focused on every day – constantly evolving and changing at the speed of changes around us, and creating a culture that is hyper-focused on unlocking customer value and experience at every turn – and reminds us how these priorities will lead to success."

**—Mike Sievert, President and CEO, T-Mobile**

"Nigel is a leading thinker on how business can transform, with unique perspectives gained from practical experience helping large and mid-size companies transform. I have worked with him and his teams on four digital transformations, spanning two decades, and know these approaches and perspectives deliver results. All that expertise is distilled into this book: It's a must-read for any leader in a company today, in any stage of your transformation journey."

**—Mittu Sridhara, Chief Technology Officer,
Careem (an Uber company)**

"The creation of personalized, seamless experiences that blur the line between physical and digital is the priority for leading businesses today. Nigel Vaz gives clear and expert advice on the strategies and capabilities necessary to help companies transform."

**—Mohamed Abdalla Al Zaabi, CEO,
Miral (Yas Island – Abu Dhabi: Warner Bros. World,
Ferrari World, Yas Waterworld)**

"*Digital Business Transformation* expertly identifies the journey through the evolution of business when – against a backdrop of immense customer and technological change – the best current and future businesses are weaving together experience, engineering and data to create new models of value. Vaz's work is an indispensable roadmap to a world that requires businesses to compete in totally new ways."

**—Riccardo Zacconi, Cofounder and Chairman,
King (creators of *Candy Crush*)**

"Nigel has evolved to become one of the best minds in the digital business space with a rich background of significant achievements as an individual and leader. He brings a powerful storytelling ability to a complex subject that many are trying to unravel and understand. This exceptional book will no doubt benefit leaders of both established businesses and start-ups."

**—Tomi Davies, Chief Investment Officer, Greentec Capital Partners and President, African Business Angels Network (ABAN); Author of *The African Project Manager***

"In *Digital Business Transformation*, Nigel Vaz sets out in writing what he and his company know and do so well: support established businesses to face their digital future by evolving what they are, what they do and how they do it. It contains all the necessary ingredients, and is a fantastic recipe for success."

**—Tony Prestedge, Deputy Chief Executive Officer, Santander UK**

"At a time when businesses are grappling with COVID on top of an ever-changing competitive landscape, *Digital Business Transformation* provides a great and timely guide for leaders to accelerate their technology-enabled business transformation. This book expertly shows how to approach transformation holistically, from rapid innovation to re-invention of the business."

**—Zaka Mian, Group Transformation Director, Lloyds Banking Group**

# DIGITAL BUSINESS TRANSFORMATION

# DIGITAL BUSINESS TRANSFORMATION

## HOW ESTABLISHED COMPANIES SUSTAIN COMPETITIVE ADVANTAGE FROM *NOW* TO *NEXT*

NIGEL VAZ

WILEY

Published by John Wiley & Sons, Inc., Hoboken, New Jersey.

Published simultaneously in Canada.



*Library of Congress Cataloging-in-Publication Data*

Names: Vaz, Nigel, author.
Title: Digital business transformation : how established companies sustain competitive advantage from now to next / Nigel Vaz.
Description: Hoboken, New Jersey : John Wiley & Sons, Inc., [2021] | Includes index.
Identifiers: LCCN 2020041518 (print) | LCCN 2020041519 (ebook) | ISBN 9781119758679 (hardback) | ISBN 9781119758662 (adobe pdf) | ISBN 9781119758686 (epub)
Subjects: LCSH: Information technology--Management. | Information technology--Economic aspects. | Organizational change. | Strategic planning.
Classification: LCC HD30.2 .V39 2021 (print) | LCC HD30.2 (ebook) | DDC 658.4/038--dc23
LC record available at https://lccn.loc.gov/2020041518
LC ebook record available at https://lccn.loc.gov/2020041519

Cover Design: Emir Orucevic
Cover Image: Publicis Sapient

SKY10022706_113020

*For my wife, Emma, my son, Ethan, my parents as well as Michelle, Darryl, Nathan, Dylan, Eric, Peter, Angela, Jen, Jo, Dan and my Publicis Groupe and Publicis Sapient family.*
*Thank you for inspiring me in everything I do.*

*"Sometimes it is the very people who no one imagines anything of who do the things no one can imagine."*

– Alan Turing

# Contents

# Preface

Organizations are reimagining, reshaping, and retooling for an era in which traditional business rules and industry frontiers have been blown wide open.

The accelerated progression of technology and its rapid uptake by consumers have pushed the issue of digital business transformation to the top of the agenda for organizations globally. The opportunity, or existential threat, that these seismic changes represent is focusing the minds of business leaders and business owners on the future of their companies and industries as never before. You may be one of them.

Every week, I am in meetings with C-level executives of some of the best-known and beloved brands in the world. Invariably, the conversation centers on the challenge of transformation: the identification of new sources of value for their customers; fending off competitive threats from digitally native entrants; learning how they too can operate with digital at the core of their business; and doing this all in an agile, iterative fashion that keeps pace with the ever-increasing rate of change in the world.

## Competitiveness and the "Digital Moat"

Warren Buffett, the CEO of Berkshire Hathaway, knows a thing or two about identifying and investing in companies with strong competitive advantage: He's built a $68 billion personal fortune off the back of that knowledge. In early 2020, Buffett lost an estimated $21 billion in net worth as a result of the economic impact of the global coronavirus pandemic yet is still understood to be the fourth richest man in the world in a list topped by Amazon founder Jeff Bezos. As we'll see, both of these are interesting asides.

The reason for our interest in Warren Buffett is that he popularized the idea of the "economic moat": the investor's approach to identifying the longevity of a business's competitive advantage.

At an annual meeting of Berkshire Hathaway shareholders, Buffett explained his principle as "trying to find a business with a wide and long-lasting moat around it, protecting a terrific economic castle with an honest lord in charge of the castle . . . it can be because it's the low-cost producer in some area, it can be because it has a natural franchise because of surface capabilities, it could be because of its position in the consumer's mind, it can be because of a technological advantage, or any kind of reason at all, that it has this moat around it."[1]

It has, as noted above, generated significant returns both for Buffett and his Berkshire Hathaway shareholders. It is, however, worth noting that the annual meeting at which he explained the "economic moat" approach was in 1995, a quarter century ago. It was in 1995 that the commercialization of the Internet really began. It was also the year in which two companies were founded: eBay and Amazon. However much the "economic moat" investment approach might have stood the test of time, it is accurate to say that it was conceived in a largely pre-digital age and, self-evidently, before Amazon set itself on a course to exceed a $1 trillion market capitalization in early 2020 and before Bezos in 2018 became the world's richest man.

What the reader of this book needs is to build and maintain their "digital moat." The following chapters are designed to help you do that. What's the difference between an "economic moat" and a "digital moat"? Certainly, they're not mutually exclusive because both focus on the development of your competitive advantage.

Warren Buffett's original "economic moat" focuses on one or a combination of moat types: low-cost production or distribution; scale; high switching costs for customers or suppliers; and intangibles, such as brand, intellectual property rights, or government regulation and licenses.

A company such as Coca-Cola has many of the qualities that define a wide economic moat. It has one of the strongest brands in the world and extraordinary geographic coverage, which adds to its awareness and customer loyalty. It also has the production advantages associated with scale (Coke and Pepsi between them control 70% of global volume in the carbonated soft drinks market), and its structural focus on producing the concentrate for drinks, rather than on the processing, bottling, and distribution gives it two advantages: lower cost and control over product quality in a taste-sensitive market. There are no high switching costs for customers here, yet the strength of Coke (and, in fact, Pepsi) is that core customers tend to remain loyal to their preferred brand regardless of price and promotion activity from their main competitor.

**A "digital moat" is the sum of the capabilities you put in place to create value and be competitive in a digital world.** It is your company's ability to evolve hard-to-duplicate, digitally supported products, services, and experiences that continually align with changing customer behaviors and technology.

A company that has one of the largest digital moats today is Amazon. It created a culture that continues to enable digital evolution through the use of agile teams with distributed decision making to the lowest part of the organization. This has created an unparalleled ability to pilot and scale adjacent products and services on its commerce platform: from its own private label goods to food delivery and even turning an internal capability, cloud computing, into an external business with Amazon Web Services.

Similarly, Uber, at its core, created an ecosystem which was based spatially around a person. Wherever you were, things could come to you. From people going to food, food could come to people. From people having to find cars, cars could come to people. From people having to interact with multiple service providers for trains, planes, buses in their vicinity, those could all now start to get connected. The Uber app digitally enabled the physical world around you and created an interface for you to engage with it. In addition, Uber created a model that attracted a supply of drivers. Through digital, drivers had an easy way to access income while enjoying the flexibility of work hours that accommodated their lives.

Both Amazon and Uber are examples of companies with wide digital moats: They were born digital and maintain their moats by being digital to their core. **This book is for established businesses who want to build their own strong digital capability through digital business transformation.** To effectively transform a business, its leaders or owners need to look at their business model as a whole and need to shift their companies or organizations significantly from where they are today.

## Why I've Written This Book

A great deal of the work I do involves meeting, advising, and helping the CEOs and leadership teams of large, established organizations on the transformation of their business for a digital age. Often, these are far more than "pre-digital businesses." The companies we work with have deep and centuries-old foundations, unparalleled industry expertise, and brand names that are not so much famous as imprinted on our collective psyche. Never mind "pre-digital," some of these organizations are "pre-electricity." This is important because they have proven, more than once, their ability to adapt to change. They have been through some of the most fundamental technological advances, generational changes in consumer behaviors and expectations, and geopolitical upheaval including world wars, macroeconomic shifts, and globalization. They have still come out on top.

Despite the proud history of these companies, their leaders recognize they have a problem and an imperative to address it. Their problem is the same as my problem, which is the same as your problem, and, in all likelihood, that of anyone who has been moved to pick up this book.

My purpose in writing this book is to help leaders get past what can be the hardest part of any personal or enterprise transformation: the choices we make every day to move toward what will drive our future success. Often, this will mean letting go of things that made us successful in the past, to make room for new skills, relationships, ways of working, and opportunities.

In this book, we decode the digital DNA of leading businesses: those things that successful companies today instinctively do or qualities they naturally possess. Decoding and understanding digital DNA is a crucial first step. It comes before transplanting that DNA into any established business.

My company, Publicis Sapient, has been in the business of digitally transforming our clients' businesses for more than 30 years. We've partnered with clients across all industries and helped them stay relevant in the digital age through the launch of the first online banks, travel portals, stock trading platforms, and retail commerce platforms. For the vast majority of those years, I have been part of that journey and it is safe to say that without Publicis Sapient, my colleagues, and our many extraordinary clients, none of what follows would have been possible.

This book is intended to help readers with the understanding and practice of transforming a business for a digital age. It is written from a practical perspective developed from decades of partnering with clients on how to take a holistic and multidisciplinary approach that infuses digital into how companies produce stronger business outcomes. The key ingredients I'll describe are your SPEED capabilities: Strategy, Product, Experience, Engineering, and Data.

I discuss many examples from the front lines of how companies defend, differentiate, or disrupt (D-3) themselves and their markets, and I try to guide leaders on how they can deconstruct decision making across every level of an organization once they embark on this journey. For most of our clients and likely the readers of this book as well, the question is no longer whether you need to transform but how. More often than not, building digital capabilities is not the hardest part of your transformation. Creating stakeholder buy-in and accountability, addressing operational process hurdles that slow decision making, and breaking down organizational silos to create a truly connected system are a much greater challenge.

## What We Mean by Digital Business Transformation

This book uses the term "digital business transformation" rather than the shorter and more generic "digital transformation." There is a good reason for this.

Often, "digital transformation" was and, for some, still is associated solely with technological change. Digital business transformation is nothing but business transformation for the digital age. Rather than digitizing parts of the business or adding some limited digital revenues as a stopgap, **the focus of this book is on how to become digital at the core: to build and sustain a digital moat that is complete, wide, and deep.** Digital business transformation is a holistic approach to changing the way an organization thinks, organizes, operates, and behaves.

Four forces of connected change are causing companies to rethink everything about how their businesses operate:

- Customer behaviors
- Technological change
- Business models
- Societal change

As disruptive technologies and companies continue to raise consumer expectations, business environments (stretching from products and services to manufacturing and marketing) are constantly changing. Digital business transformation closes the gap between what consumers expect and what their traditional business models can deliver.

Digital business transformation is a journey that trumps its destination, a journey that asks businesses to reimagine and rapidly realize new ways of working and satisfying consumer expectations. It has a slightly different meaning for each organization and uses different tools to address the unique challenges of each business. Most important, digital business transformation could mean the difference between an organization surviving the next five years or not.

## COVID-19 Taught Us How to Change Faster

This book begins with a deliberate emphasis on change: its nature and its speed. As we'll see, change was and is exponential even before COVID-19 came along to devastatingly illustrate how rapidly change occurs in today's world. Coronavirus is the defining, shared episode of almost all adult readers' business lives. That is not to make light of the pandemic, for it is as great a human tragedy as most of us will ever experience.

From a business perspective, it has acted as an accelerant in the wholesale transformation of business relationships and interactions between companies, customers, suppliers, and employees. This speed and impact were neatly summed up by Microsoft CEO Satya Nadella, when he observed: "As COVID-19 impacts every aspect of our work and life, we have seen two years' worth of digital transformation in two months."[2]

As an interesting if morbid aside, when the Black Death spread across Europe and into Asia and Africa, it did so at an average 1.5 kilometres a day. Why? Because that plague occurred in the fourteenth century when the most common form of locomotion was walking, and the fastest was on the back of a horse. The Black Death is known to have spread through the maritime and land trading routes of the time, which, although well established, were slow. COVID-19 spreads at approximately 926 km per hour (or 575 mph), the speed at which infected passengers might be traveling on a long-distance commercial passenger aircraft.

COVID-19 magnified the rate of change in the world around us, including the business environment. Countries, companies, and individuals rapidly moved from seeking to protect health to adapting our work and our lives to this new context: Challenges in our existing infrastructure and processes became apparent, but so too did opportunities to do things differently and, potentially, better than before.

Who would have thought that within the space of a few short weeks the employees of many businesses around the world would be working from home? That those would be the fortunate ones and elsewhere hundreds of millions of people would be laid off from work or furloughed, and that, as a consequence, governments would be paying their wages, experimenting with universal basic income, or rolling out record-breaking financial stimulus packages? That industry events globally as well as public gatherings generally would be canceled? That schools would be closed and a third of the global population would be on some form of coronavirus lockdown at home?

Coronavirus has had a profound and unprecedented impact on the way we behave, on how we interact socially, how we consume, and how we work. It illustrates our shared humanity in the most visceral way. It shows that our similarities are greater than our differences, while also exposing the gaps between the rich and the poor, between those with privilege and those without. It is an experience that resonates across borders and impacts individuals, small and large companies alike, and industries in their entirety.

You may now be thinking that we are all aware of the existential impact of coronavirus on companies and people across the world and the need to transform, but other than providing a more recent context, why is it important for digital business transformation?

With the spread of COVID-19 globally, what is being witnessed is the exponential rate of change. You could see change rapidly happening around you and react to it as it was happening. Companies, as well as public institutions such as schools, did not have the luxury of waiting a few weeks to see what happened: They had to absorb imperfect information as it came in and react immediately, while also planning for long-term implications.

Now what happens when the changes happening around us are not as obvious or, in some cases, seem invisible? That's exactly what's happening to established businesses as it relates to technological change. Technology is, in fact, advancing at an exponential rate. For companies built to identify and harness that change, they can apply it in the context of consumer needs better and faster than incumbent brands, leaving those not equipped for that context left to react. That is the crux of the divide between digitally native companies and established businesses and what this book is designed to address.

On the other side of all this, there will be a responsibility and, yes, an opportunity to assess and define what business looks like in a post-COVID world. Where emerging technologies and disruptive business models were pushing organizations to digitally transform, coronavirus has forced the immediate adoption of new ways of working and of channels to connect with customers, the best of which will remain once the pandemic has gone.

Coronavirus came along and effectively, if tragically, illustrated the interconnectedness of human behavior, emerging technologies, business models, and societal impact in a way that could not have been predicted. In its way, unpredictability is rather the point.

## What This Book Will Do for You

The intent and design of *Digital Business Transformation* is to assist the reader in doing just that, putting in place a set of organizational capabilities and ways of working that in turn drive the business outcomes that will make your company or organization relevant and competitive in a digital world.

While *Digital Business Transformation* is written with C-suite leaders of established businesses in mind, it is also very much a road map for every level of business person and business type: from the large to the small and medium-sized enterprises. At its heart, this book decodes the qualities and traits (or the DNA) of leading digital businesses and explains what established businesses need to do in order to replicate those qualities, an opportunity open to large "pre-digital" businesses as well as to smaller companies that are starting out or scaling up.

*Digital Business Transformation* is divided into three parts: Now, Next, and How.

Part One, "Now", explores companies' present state and the context: a world where the rate of change is exponential and the forces of change are connected and happening all at once. The key takeaway from these chapters is a better understanding of the nature and scale of change that you are facing, and the ability to identify the brakes and blocks that are holding your business back.

Part Two, "Next", shines a light on companies' future state: decoding what leading digital companies do well and how they do it, and what is required of established businesses in order to build their own digital moat. In "Next", you will discover the six factors necessary to the creation of a digital organization. These are the SPEED capabilities of Strategy, Product, Experience, Engineering, and Data, as well as the ability to think and behave differently and become a "Gryphon organization."

How do you get from "Now" to "Next"? The third and final part of this book is "How". It provides the reader with different transformation paths, depending on your business need and situation, and insight into attributes of successful digital business transformation programs.

# SECTION 1

# NOW

# CHAPTER 1

# The Death of Business as Usual

## It's All Change

Change is not what it used to be. The business leaders of today, and those of tomorrow, will find it much harder than their predecessors to face down challenges and respond to change. This is not due to any personal limitations on their part. It's quite the opposite.

John D. Rockefeller, Andrew Carnegie, and Henry Ford all had it easy compared with the reader of this book. For them, business challenges came sequentially. They were experiencing linear change, which, while significant, was of an entirely different magnitude than the effect of all the change happening at once: human behavior, emerging technology, and the availability of funds and investment to create entirely different business models. For them, change did not accelerate away more quickly than it was humanly possible to chase, comprehend, and to adapt.

In the early years of the twentieth century, when Rockefeller, Carnegie, and Ford were building their business empires and amassing their fortunes, the term "CEO" was an abbreviation for "Chief Electricity Officer" rather than "Chief Executive Officer" as it is today. This reflected the fact that electricity was a business-critical technology that warranted its own leadership function within the organization. It was a linear change, with a specific solution. As will likely be the case with the "Chief Digital Officer" of today, the role of Chief Electricity

Officer was transitory and disappeared as soon as it became apparent that their specialty, in fact, sat at the heart of and powered the entire organization.

Not all established businesses are successful at riding the wave of change. We all know the stories of Blockbuster, Kodak, Nokia, and a host of other legacy businesses and we won't be revisiting those cases in this book. Even those businesses didn't fail absolutely and, for the most part, did not entirely disappear – it is even possible to visit the last remaining Blockbuster store in operation the next time you're passing through Bend, Oregon.

What those companies did allow to happen to them was to be outmaneuvered by digitally native entrants to their markets and to lose their once dominant position in those markets. Nokia didn't "fail" in the mobile phone market. Having started life as a paper mill in 1865, it made successful leaps through electricity, rubber, cable, and communications to later own more than 50% of global market share of smartphones. When it needed to leap again, Nokia stalled and stumbled. It wasn't able to build a platform business or to surround itself with an expansive ecosystem of apps, content, information, and entertainment. Its digital moat had dried up and it was unable to resist the incursions of new competitors. It was a manufacturing company in, to paraphrase the entrepreneur, investor, and engineer Marc Andreessen, a world being eaten by software. It was outmaneuvered, principally by Apple.

## Truth, Knowledge, Vision

The American Museum of Natural History is an extraordinary building in many ways. The largest natural history museum in the world, it houses one of the most important records of life on earth. For anyone seeking answers to the bigger questions, such as the significance or not of human evolution in space and time, then they are surely to be found hidden among the 33 million-odd specimens spread across the museum's two million square feet. The museum acted as a magnet does to the insatiable curiosity of a boy growing up in Manhattan – a constant and irresistible attraction.

My son, as many boys do, from an early age had a relentless fascination with dinosaurs. From home on the Upper East Side of New York City, the quickest route to the museum is a run-walk across Central

Park and a few quick bounds up the steps and in through the Central Park West entrance, otherwise known as the Theodore Roosevelt Memorial Hall. Ignore for now, as he invariably did, the words "Truth, Knowledge, Vision" that are thoughtfully inscribed above the Roman-style entrance pillars. Inside, after all, there are dinosaurs to be seen.

The centerpiece of the Theodore Roosevelt Rotunda is the life-size cast of a female Barosaurus rearing up on her hind legs to defend her young against the incoming attack of a fearsome Allosaurus. It has to be one of the most spectacular dinosaur exhibits anywhere in the world. It is storytelling using protagonists brought to life from the late Jurassic period, 150 million or so years ago. It is also huge. Owing to its tripod-rearing position, the Barosaurus (AMNH 6341) is, at 50 feet, the world's tallest freestanding dinosaur exhibit. As your gaze tracks up the vertebrae to the skull, you may wonder whether it is taller than those beautiful red marble Corinthian columns that anchor the room. It is, by a couple of feet. Having been temporarily distracted by the majestic architecture, you may even wonder whether you could set another Barosaurus on top of this one and still fit it within the soaring octagonal coffered, barrel-vaulted ceiling. You could, but only just.

It is truly an awe-inspiring display, in one of the most graceful architectural settings. Or, as the museum Trustees better described it, "a conception of the grandeur and dignity . . . which elevates the emotions and impresses the soul as but few of the monuments to man have ever done." It is unfortunate then, that, in the scenario we're soon to depict, we must flood the space in order to illustrate a point.[1]

Before we do that, though, let's leave the Sauropod behind and leap forward to just 1.9 million years ago and to the emergence of Homo erectus. For most of those 1.9 million years, our primary form of locomotion has been bipedal or walking upright. Figure 1.1 shows that in a time line of land-based transportation, for all but 0.3% of that time line walking has been our sole means of getting from one place to the next. Only at around 5,500 years ago did we begin to ride on the backs of animals, which was fairly quickly followed by the invention and use of the wheel. Man and beast, cart and coach, then seemingly plodded along quite happily until the seventeenth and eighteenth centuries.[2]

Of all the activity and invention that brought about and defined the Industrial Revolution, we've selected just two inventions to drop into our time line. The first is Thomas Newcomen's "atmospheric steam engine" of 1711, not the first steam engine but arguably the most important as it both enabled the profitable extraction of coal

**FIGURE 1.1** History of land-based transportation

from flooded mines and, many iterations later, powered pretty much everything including the transportation of people. The second is Carl Benz's Motorwagen, which, in 1885, became the first car to realistically be powered by the internal combustion engine. Returning to our land-based transportation time line, these two developments, respectively, would occupy 0.016% and 0.007% of its length.

Tesla was founded in 2003, and Uber in 2009. These represent the most significant recent disruptions to our understanding of land-based transportation. They were not the first in their fields, but became dominant players: despite the existence of other electric cars, Tesla's made popular impact while Uber's significance was to deliver ride-sharing on a global scale.

Tesla has disrupted the notion that the combustion engine will power the future. More importantly, Tesla thinks of and markets the car as a platform, so that people can now effectively download their car. Uber has come along and posed the questions "Isn't the purpose of cars to transport things and people connected?" and "Why do we even need cars to be owned? Why can't we actually just share them?" And so this automotive, or mobility, industry that itself represents no more than a sliver on the time line of human locomotion, has witnessed two of its biggest consumer disruptions in just the past 18 years. And what percentage of the transportation time line does 18 years occupy? Just 0.0009%.

The point of this industry-specific example is that the speed, scale, and significance of the change taking place all around us is real, not imagined. That's without factoring in driverless cars and passenger drones, the impact of which may be at least as profound. Whether you're operating in the mobility industry or not hardly matters. What we are witnessing is a rate of change unlike anything experienced before. This is forcing every single industry to reevaluate itself.

The transformation of business and industries is not a new phenomenon. Those stovepipe-hatted engineers and inventors of the Industrial Revolution were harnessing and evolving the technologies of their age at a pace that must have appeared wondrous to the people of the time. The reason that digital is so significant for our age is that it signifies the coming together of rapid change in consumer behavior, technology, business models, and a growing awareness of the impact that business and technology has on societies and our environment. Together, these four forces are driving disruptive change.

You may be familiar with Ray Kurzweil's "Law of Accelerating Returns", often cited because few have better made the case that technological evolution is exponential and not linear. In it, he argues that the current paradigm shift rate (rate of technical progress) doubles roughly every decade, so the rate of acceleration is growing exponentially. As such, the technological progress we will make in the twenty-first century alone is a thousand times greater than was the case in the twentieth century. Delivered in linear form, that is without the doubling of paradigm shift rates, the technological progress we will witness in this century, would have taken around 20,000 years.

Standing on the sidelines with your Internet-enabled mobile phone, this accelerating rate of change can be a tricky thing to grasp. You haven't quite come to grips with that phone's full functionality yet, but you'll catch up, right?[3]

So, how do we begin to comprehend what exponential growth looks like compared with linear? Kurzweil uses grains of rice on the squares of a chess board. We, however, will return to the Theodore Roosevelt Rotunda at the American Museum of Natural History which, since we were there last, has sprung a leak.

The highly polished marble floor of this grand, John Russell Pope -designed room measures 67 feet wide by 120 feet long. Its curved ceiling, as we have learned, stretches to a maximum height of 100 feet. The first droplet of water to hit the floor, then, barely registers within the hall's capacious 698,000 cubic feet. Even though the drops of water keep coming, in linear fashion, at a rate of one per second, there is no cause for alarm. It will take another 26,006 years for a full puddle to form at the feet of our Barosaurus and another 4,074 centuries for the water to close over her head. In 752,589 years the hall will be completely flooded.

Now, grab a metaphorical towel or, better still, some scuba gear and let's see what happens if the rate of water droplets entering the room increases exponentially – one drop, two drops, four drops . . . Even if she could calculate $X(t)= x_0 \times (1 + r)^t$, it's unlikely that the mathematical solution would matter as much to our Barosaurus as the solution that has rapidly been filling the room and which has now closed over her head . . . after just 38 minutes. In less than a minute, the hall will be filled to bursting point. Here's the thing though – just 10 minutes earlier the water had been no more than about a four-inch-deep puddle on the floor.

The Barosaurus has an excuse for remaining immobile throughout both scenarios, being, as she is, a life-size cast skeleton. What about you? A sentient and smart human being? From the facts that water was swirling at your feet and that the leak had not been plugged but seemed to be getting bigger, could you have deduced the escalating severity of the situation? Almost certainly not.

It is human nature to observe the current rate of change and assume that rate will extend into the future. Even when we are ankle-deep in the empirical evidence of an increasing rate of change, it is nearly impossible to project what that will mean in a future period. Our most recent experiences and our perceived success at adapting to those experiences fool us into believing that we can see what the future holds and make a plan for it.

Truth, Knowledge, Vision. Those three words above the entrance to the American Museum of Natural History – they're important here, too. The purpose of the museum is to understand our planet and the known universe and, through ongoing research, to discover more and correct past assumptions. That's the "Truth." Then there's "Knowledge," which the museum imparts in the most compelling ways: through experience and education.

What about "Vision" though? Vision is not something you would immediately associate with a museum, trading, as they generally do, in all things historic. I like to think, though, that the architects of the American Museum of Natural History knew what they were about. That they had a vision for what they were trying to create in the world. The past is not a great predictor of the future, but it does create the context to help you envisage a better future.

What the past gives us is truth, knowledge, and an understanding of the world around us, our place in it, and our extraordinary advantage as a species to adapt to change and circumstance. Is there any better place from which to start?

## Constant Beta

Digital business transformation is akin to permanent disruption, a self-imposed regimen that recognizes transformation not as a one-and-done endeavor but as an ongoing commitment to adapt in line with changing customer needs and shifting industry landscapes.

One of the most powerful shifts in business over the past decade is value creation. While successful established businesses have always been value-centric, for most of their existence businesses have created value with some combination of their core products and services, brand, economies of scale, and efficiencies. These were the sources of competitive advantage identified by Warren Buffett as the basis for companies' "economic moat." The challenge now is that these traditional sources of value that determined the width of that moat are no longer sufficient to sustain the advantage.

As a parent, one of the lessons I reiterate with my son is that what you know is not as important as your desire and ability to learn. For a 10-year-old boy, the advice is pretty straightforward and a restless curiosity makes it easy to follow. For established businesses, however, which may have had decades of success built on well-established processes and ways of working, breaking from the rigidity of "what you know" is far more challenging.

Perhaps the most foundational component of building a digital moat is creating the ability for your organization to learn, unlearn, and relearn. For established businesses, this requires a shift from a product mindset to a software mindset. Traditionally, product companies think linearly with a clear beginning and end to product development. Software development and management, on the other hand, is continuous and ever evolving, adding new functionality and changes as a reaction to customer, business, and market demands. This allows a more rapid response to the rate and scale of change in consumer expectations.

## Digital Assets and Liabilities

Once you have a vision of what your differentiated future business model can look like, one of the biggest questions to answer is: what capabilities should we invest in? What are the capabilities that are the essence of what it means to be digital? These are not just the technologies you think will underpin the future; they are robust, evolving capability categories that will define you as a company in the future. They are your assets and your identity as a digital organization, your SPEED capabilities: Strategy, Product, Experience, Engineering, and Data.

Long gone are the days when a company's primary orientation to technology and digital can be thought of from a cost perspective. As assets, they are part and parcel of how you create value for your customers and in the market. A few years back, at a series of "Idea Exchange" events that Publicis Sapient was hosting for clients and partners, I spent time with "molecular gastronomy" chef Heston Blumenthal and film director James Cameron. What struck me was that each of them, perhaps more than others in their respective fields at the time, were pushing at the envelope of what technology allowed them to create and how it changed the rules of not only what was possible but what was expected of their peers and by their "customers."

Heston Blumenthal was not classically trained and sometimes found himself belittled by critics for not being a "proper chef" and for being over-reliant on technology. "But fire is technology, an oven is technology," he said. "People thought it was strange that I was using a centrifuge in my kitchen. They all use a blender today, but once upon a time that would have seemed like cutting edge technology." Today, Blumenthal has expanded his relationship with technology from how it can be applied to the making of food to the role that innovations like virtual reality and robotics can play in the experience of food.

James Cameron explained how in order to make the movies *The Abyss* and later *Avatar* – for which he had already had the creative vision – he had to wait for the necessary technology to be invented, and, in specific circumstances, to invent it himself. In the case of *Avatar,* this included not just advancements in filmmaking and graphics that you may naturally associate with the movie. Cameron partnered with Microsoft to create Gaia, a cloud-based platform that processed and gave the movie's distributed team access to the massive amounts of data being generated for the film. Gaia became so critical to the movie, producer Jon Landau said, "Without Gaia, we would not have been able to do the production. Gaia was the backbone that everything else ran on top of."[4]

If there's a lesson here, it's to have a vision of the value you want to create in the world and then use not just technology, but the breadth of your digital capabilities to realize that value. In this way, digital becomes more than an enabler, it becomes an asset. And, as we'll explore in future chapters, like the creation of *Avatar,* that asset may go beyond your walls to the ecosystem of partners that will expand what's possible for your business.

In turn, you can't advance your assets without also taking an honest look at your digital liabilities. These include both the tangible and intangible aspects of your business that stand in the way of your ability to keep pace with consumer behavior and expectations. Many established businesses have structures and processes in place that wrongly put the emphasis on the scope and outputs of projects rather than on the outcomes for the business. This creates what's known as "technical debt," where those companies take what appears to be the easier, shorter path instead of the path that will produce the right outcomes.

The questions facing many businesses are similar: what to do about legacy technology investment, how to connect disparate datasets to create a single view of the customer, and (one of the most challenging shifts), how to break down functional silos that were originally designed to support your legacy organization? How will you change your orientation now that the primary focus of your technology investment is not just cost and risk, but value and differentiation? How will you pivot away from what made your business successful in the past to what will make it successful going forward?

There was a moment when digital became an inextricable part of the human experience. Some might say it was the adoption of the Internet, many that it was the invention of the iPhone. Seeing what was happening was not the challenge. Recognizing the speed with which it would develop and knowing how to keep pace was (and still is).

Think back to our friend the Barosaurus, standing stoically as drops of water filled the room around her at an increasing rate until she quickly becomes engulfed. At any given point, it could be seen that the water level was rising, yet at some point the room went rapidly from being merely wet to being flooded. With the exponential flow rate, even if you tried to open the doors, at some point the pressure would become so great that merely reacting to the situation would not be enough. You would have to adapt.

While many companies saw the rise of digital over the years, there were few who invested in it early. Many thought (or still think) of digital as tangential to their core business. Yet the shift of digital from being tangential to being existential is no longer about any singular technology or innovation; it's about how consumer behavior and expectations have and will continue to change as a result of digital and whether a company is influencing that change or reacting to it.

## Digital Business Transformation: Why It's More Than Just Technology

What's particularly challenging for established businesses is that acquiring technological capabilities alone will not be sufficient to create the kind of moats you see surrounding the most successful digital companies. The competitive advantage of digital companies comes from their integrated set of capabilities, what they are able to create with those capabilities, and the cultural principles that underpin the systems that create their outputs. Digitally native companies consistently challenge established brands in platform business models, network effects, convenience, agility, and customer experience. These are the outcomes of their "digital moat" – the competitive advantage created through their digital capability.

While it is one thing to talk about the digital moats of digitally native companies, changing an established organization's orientation to how they create value is incredibly daunting. One recent example is the Walt Disney Company's launch of Disney+. Bob Iger, Disney's CEO, had spoken about the importance and challenge of maintaining "relevance" and being open to disrupting yourself, even when that means changing some of the foundational aspects of what made you successful to begin with.[5] With Disney+, the company disrupted the licensing, sales, and distribution of their most core asset: their content. To enable this new model, in 2018 Disney announced a reorganization of the business, placing the management of their direct-to-consumer distribution platforms, technology, and international operations under a single leader to support not only Disney+, but ESPN+ and Hulu through more connected technology, data, and experience capabilities. The integration of these capabilities surfaced greater customer insights that enabled more personalization and improved user experiences.[6]

When Disney+ was launched in 2019, Disney projected it would have between 60 million and 90 million subscribers by 2024. However, by May of 2020, it had 54.5 million, accelerated by demand from the COVID-19 pandemic.[7] By comparison, Hulu was reporting 32.1 million subscribers and Netflix reported 182.9 million internationally. During the 2020 Q2 earnings call, when the COVID crisis shut down revenue from its parks and cruises, Disney reported positive overall growth, much of which was attributed to the new Disney+ business model.[8]

What Disney did was to launch a successful digital streaming business, which now increases its relevance. But that was also only one step in creating a competitive digital capability. Disney will be taking on the challenge of evolving their new subscription-based streaming service, the consumer content demands associated with the likes of Netflix, and creating an experience that reflects their brand and meets the expectations of consumers over time. From here on, Disney+ will need to nurture and support an operating model that will continuously evolve and create value over time.

### DBT Takeaway: The Death of Business as Usual

There is a reason I've dedicated a whole chapter of this book to the idea of exponential change, and it's this. Until business leaders – of established organizations, as well as of (for now) the disruptive digital natives – understand and accept the speed, scale, and significance of the change taking place all around us, they are at its mercy and most certainly are not in control.

The purpose of this book is to help you to do two things. We'll see later how these two Big Hairy Audacious Goals (BHAGs) sit at the heart of any successful business transformation:

- To create an organization that is able to continually change at a pace that matches the changes around it.
- To build the capability to identify and realize value for your customers and business through digital.

Digital business transformation helps to set you on the path to operate in this space of permanent disruption. Your key factors for success:

- Focus on your organization's ability (and willingness) to learn, unlearn, and relearn. Look at your company as being in a state of constant beta.
- Understand the capabilities that will define you as a company in the future. They are your assets and your identity as a digital organization, your SPEED capabilities: Strategy, Product, Experience, Engineering, and Data.

Recognize that competitive advantage does not come from technological capabilities alone: it comes from an integrated set of capabilities, what you are able to create with those capabilities, and a culture that embraces change.

# CHAPTER 2

# The Four Forces of Connected Change

On the occasion of the 25th anniversary of the World Wide Web, back in 2014, I spoke at an event alongside its inventor, Sir Tim Berners-Lee. Berners-Lee is the British scientist at CERN who, in 1989, wrote the lines of code that connected the seminal components that produce the web we know today. Sir Tim and I talked *around* the World Wide Web rather than specifically about it. We explored ideas and issues including the augmentation of human mental and cognitive faculties, how programmatic decision making would disrupt supply chains, how the business-consumer relationship around low-emotion purchases would be disintermediated by technology, and how data would be expropriated – wrestled back by consumers from governments and corporations.

It's extraordinary to think, today, about how the breadth of these topics all centered on one invention: the web. Today, digital has extended well beyond Sir Tim's invention, while at the same time being underpinned by it. And, talking about the impact of digital on businesses can feel similar to our conversation: at once both awe-inspiring and intimidating.

Understanding the impact of digital on your business starts with taking a deeper look at the four forces that, together, are changing the context in which you operate:

- customer behaviors,
- technological change,
- business models, and
- societal impact.

It is the very nature of these four forces of connected change that movement in one can affect any or all of the others. Each of these forces is undergoing radical change in and of themselves, but combined, they are fundamentally changing the commercial landscape. Understanding this context will help you identify your business's core strengths, as well as those areas where it is weak and susceptible to the market forces that disrupt so many businesses today.

# Customer Behaviors

"The customer is always right" is a phrase that long precedes the digital age. It harks back to an era in which the customer may have been "right" but most definitely was not in charge. What has changed, and is always changing, is the power that customers now hold in their relationship with companies and brands. In part, this is due to a general shift in power dynamics between companies and their customers. In part, it is due to technology perpetually enabling consumers to do and to expect more and, most importantly, give customers a "digital megaphone" to amplify their perspective on the organizations they do business with.

## The Shifting Power Balance to Consumers

Today, convenience, personalization, and experience are key measures of customer value and can be what distinguishes established companies from leading digital businesses. Customers, using digital sources to make their purchasing decision, expect things to be connected, secure, and easy to use; for brand experiences to be "frictionless" and to work, flow, and center on their daily lives; that products and services will make their lives simpler and more rewarding; and for technology to work in a seamless way. On top of this, they don't perceive or expect a difference between online and offline; to them it's all one world, and it's their world.

That all sounds a bit self-centered, and it is. The balance of power has moved from companies to customers, whose expectations of how, where, and when their needs are met have all risen dramatically. Those leading digital businesses that are able to exceed these customer expectations set a new benchmark. That new benchmark soon becomes the baseline by which the efforts of established businesses and the traditional practices of entire industries are judged.

In the past that would have mattered less, as the behaviors and expectations were largely defined and driven by companies. The Henry Ford quote that "any customer can have a car painted any color that he wants so long as it is black" spoke to this traditional production-oriented way of thinking. In fact, that quote was preceded by a more telling – if slightly less "colorful" – passage: "In 1909, I announced one morning, without any previous warning, that in the future we were going to build only one model, that the model was going to be 'Model T,' and that the chassis would be exactly the same for all cars."[1]

Efficiency is still a primary focus for CEOs, but mass production is no longer pursued at the expense of customer choice. To do business in this way today, by rigidly making one or a few products that meet the needs of an imagined homogeneous customer base, would be risky business. The rules have changed.

Today, we work and live in the age of the customer. A large part of this shift in power from companies to consumers is rooted in the advances of digital technology and the information revolution those have brought about.

## Ecosystem Evolution

Emerging digital technologies have run in parallel with, and accelerated, this consumer boom and have turned the corporate-consumer dynamic on its head. We have moved from a post-war period, where businesses dictated production and used mass media to broadcast their promotional messages, to one in which customers have access to a vastly greater amount of information on product and pricing and the ability to share information, recommendations, and negative reviews across their virtual spheres of influence.

In the digital age, one of the biggest shifts happening is ecosystem evolution, where the best experiences that consumers have define the experiences they have across other sectors. Any experience that you have in one place affects the context of everywhere else.

One example is banks, where competitive advantage historically centered on trust but where digital has rapidly increased the importance of convenience. The reason that customers get frustrated at having to stand in a line to provide the identification that will allow them to open a bank account is not because that process has become more cumbersome over time. It is because other experiences have become easier and quicker, such as an Uber driver finding you and taking you to your destination at the click of a button.

Similarly, the preferred airline of a customer will know where they would like to sit on the plane, what they will or won't eat, can check them in online, and fast-track them through the airport. This makes the experience of then arriving at the hotel brand of choice, and waiting around to be checked in on three different systems only to be allocated the room they have available rather than the one you'd prefer, incredibly frustrating. Again, it's not the hotel chain that has made things slower or less personal; it's that the customer's experiences elsewhere have redefined what good and bad look like. Your "competitors" aren't necessarily even in the same industry sector as you.

In this ecosystem, customers have a connected, symbiotic relationship with each other that has fundamentally changed the nature of their relationship with companies and brands. These customers communicate with and influence each other and have it in their power to make or break the reputation of businesses.

In this context, it is understandable that customers are less loyal than they used to be. They are susceptible to being lured away by the superior, intuitive experiences offered elsewhere. The digital tools they have in hand allow them instant access to information in a transparent and democratized marketplace that aids their own purchasing decision, and allows them to influence the purchasing decisions of others.

## Technological Change

Do you remember where you learned about the targeted military operation and death of Osama Bin Laden? No, I didn't think so. The raid on the Al-Qaeda leader's hideout in Pakistan was months in the planning but completed within 40 minutes in the early hours of May 2, 2011. One of the first people to be aware that something was happening – outside a tight US military circle, that is – was IT engineer Sohaib Athar. In the wee hours of that morning, he Tweeted, "Helicopter hovering above Abbottabad at 1am (is a rare event)." Then, minutes later, "A huge window-shaking bang here in Abbottabad. I hope it's not the start of something nasty."[2] In that moment, many of the world's news organizations, some centuries old, were being scooped to a news story of such magnitude by a guy on Twitter.

A client of ours, one of the largest media companies in the world with a range of world-famous newspaper brands, had been alert to its new reality for some years before the Bin Laden raid. In the digital age – when breaking news traveled around the globe in an instant, and was as likely to be disseminated by Twitter as by rival organizations – our client's ways of working no longer represented competitive advantage.

The client needed a way to operate in a world where consumer technology was now enabling citizen journalism. But they needed to do so while maintaining the integrity and reputation they had built over centuries. Publicis Sapient partnered with them to create a "breaking views" proposition that shifted both how they used technology to deliver news while introducing new ways of working within their organization to adapt to the changing world around them.

The proposition was rooted in our client's long-standing reputation for reporting world events while giving no-holds-barred opinion and the context behind the story. On one level this was "just" a cross-channel delivery platform that connected newsprint, web, and mobile. At a deeper, more fundamental level, it involved addressing the emerging technologies and resulting customer behavior changes. It also required shifting the culture of an established organization and its ways of working. From "news" on paper to "views" online. This involved changing the culture and ways of working for journalists and a cycle of publishing once every 24 hours to one of posting news and comments live online.

The rapid rate of technological progress sits at the heart of the transformation imperative. Technology is the enabler that allows businesses to identify and unlock customer value and to connect with them. However, it is also what bends the competitive context out of shape.

Technology is impacting every facet of business today: not just on how we meet customers' expectations but also the nature of who our competitors are and where they come from. It's changing how we create efficiencies within our businesses and industries, how we bring products and services to market at speed, and how we gather information and understanding of our customers.

It is human endeavor that develops technology and, in turn, technology drives forward human endeavor. It is worth noting that there is nothing new about the creation and use of technology to develop new products or services, or to advance the ease, speed, and scale of production. Harnessing the power of animals for agriculture and transportation, the wheel, the evolving power sources of water, steam, and electricity – these are all technological leaps that have driven business and society forward. They are leaps that have created monumentally successful businesses for those that realized their potential, but failures among those who resisted or rejected change.

One of the most significant of these shifts, the electrification of businesses, took around 40 years, spanning the end of the nineteenth century through to the 1930s. The same calculations, of risk and cost, were made by business leaders back then as now. The same experiments were carried out of adding electricity to their businesses incrementally before it became easier (and obvious) to put electricity at the core of everything they did. The technology was a fundamental shift, but in terms of the rate of change it was linear. You would have had to go out of your way to get left behind over a period of 40 years. Today, it can happen in the blink of an eye.

To revisit Kurzweil, his point that "few observers have truly internalized the implications of the fact that rate of change itself is accelerating" is highly applicable to the business environment and an inability to keep pace either with technological advances or the change to the competitive context that those advances are bringing about.

## Technology and the Customer Experience

The most important technological change of our time is not any individual technology but the central role technology plays in the lives of consumers.

While the evolution of digital technologies has impacted both consumers and enterprises, it is what has been put in the hands of the individual that is the origin of the real revolution: whether that person is a consumer sitting in their home or an employee at work in their company's offices. For our purposes, the first significant cycle came with personal computing in its broadest sense. Having a computer at home, and in the office, allowed more people to perform more tasks and functions more efficiently and productively than at any time in human history.

In short order, possession of a personal computer was followed by a succession of technological waves that have increasingly made technology a systemically important part of our lives, of commerce, and of society. Connectivity brought those PCs together – in both a literal and physical sense – so that we became networked within the institutional and office environments and then, through the Internet, became connected at home. The acceleration in computing power, in parallel with a rapidly and radically improving interface, further advanced the functionality and usability of these technologies. The progression of mobility – both in terms of the devices and the ability to connect anywhere – has freed us to choose how and where we work, access information, and form relationships and communicate with others.

If there is an additional wave, or layer, to add it is the free-to-use platforms that have enhanced our abilities and experiences in the digital world, whether from a social or work perspective – as well as increasing the number of hours we spend online. These include ad-based platforms such as Facebook and YouTube, as well as those that give away some functionality for free such as Google Docs or Zoom (daily usage of which has increased by more than 300% since the COVID-19 pandemic struck). Taken together, these advances have driven and expanded our digital world and placed technology at the center of our day-to-day experience.

Yet, how many established companies have technology at the center of their businesses? For most, it is still a tangential idea: it may get significant investment and advance products and services, but it has not yet become core to the working model or decision making. And even with investment, there is the pre-existing challenge of deciding what to do with legacy technologies currently running the business. For established businesses, one of the biggest challenges is knowing what to let go of and what to keep. The cultural and technological underpinnings of established companies are often the biggest determinants of whether they are reactive instead of proactive with regards to technological change, and in effect to changes to the customer experience and expectations.

## The Role of Data

While hardware, software, and connectivity are all driving technology's impact on consumers, one of the biggest technology challenges and opportunities for companies is around data.

Many organizations used to (and some still do) think about data as something that existed in the context of a particular function. That is the way in which their tools were enabled: customer relationship management (CRM) tools gather and utilize CRM data, online sales tools generate online sales data. There was very little understanding that data is all about enabling the people that interact with it: The data could be connected across functions, in the context of the customer journey or to empower people internally who were using it to more quickly make changes to the business.

As a result, most types of data, from sales and marketing to financial, were both very functional and a reflection of the organizational silos that existed within a business. When company leaders step back and, instead of obsessing over how they operate their business, orient from the perspective of how customers interact with them, then having all these pieces of data that often relate to the same customer, but housing them in a completely disconnected environment, makes no sense at all.

The reason that organizations have not made as much progress in this vein before now is that they neither had the technology nor the organizational perspective to be able to do anything with that data in a meaningful way. In the past, a marketing department trying to upsell or cross-sell to an existing customer in a particular area with a promotional discount may have been unaware that the same customer is frustrated by, and has even reported, a fault in the system that is negatively affecting their experience. To that customer your new promotion seems a completely disconnected way for the company to be interacting with them.

That disconnect is largely a result of the way the systems were organized and the functional separation that exists. Today, customers are a lot less tolerant of it and organizations recognize the need to understand that customer in a more rounded sense. They benefit in their ability to retain that customer in the longer term, to upsell or cross-sell more effectively.

The major technological shift has been from the functional separation of data toward systems that allow data to flow in an abstracted fashion, the creation of middleware technology platforms that connect data in a more meaningful way in the context of a customer journey. Prior to this, most processes in IT systems were hard-coded, with all the logic for what a company should do in marketing, for example, hard-coded into a marketing system because those were the tools that enable those functions.

Today, organizations recognize that it is fine to have systems to deal with specific situations in customer service or in marketing, but what is not fine is not being able to leverage what's happening in those systems and connect the dots across the organization to serve the customer's needs.

Cloud computing was designed to provide computing power and storage in what is essentially a connected environment. The three ideas that underpin the cloud are significant because they have allowed cloud-based systems to evolve to mean a great deal more to businesses today. These are: cheap storage because it's easier to store information centrally; computation so you have real computing power behind the storage; and finally, and most importantly, the ability to access the information and to be connected from wherever you were.

The idea of outsourcing non-core functions has been an important aspect of business management for many, many years. Yet a host of digital tools today are a relatively recent addition to the business leader's armory, and they have changed the nature of how companies operate. When technology eliminates the assumption that you have to build and operate every infrastructural component yourself, it allows a company to focus on where and how they can create the most value.

Reduced management emphasis on the need to build each and every component of your company's "factory" allows more time to focus on what your core competence is about. Unfortunately, while this is a benefit to you, it is also of benefit to newer, agile digital competitors and their ability to enter your market.

The digital technologies available today allow every player, from established businesses to digital start-ups, to have an improved and connected understanding of customer needs and behaviors, and the ability to serve those customers with relevant products and services. What defines success for any company now is less the technologies available, and more their organization's capacity to identify and harness the technologies that best serve a clear vision of their own offering to add value for the customer and, in turn, the business.

## Business Models

If yours is an organization whose business was founded, and is based, on a pre-digital model then the rapid advances in technology and their take-up, by consumers as well as by competitors, present particular challenges.

First, you have to decide what and how to transform and, in the process of that transformation, to determine which technologies to invest in in order to defend your position, to differentiate from competitors, or even to disrupt yourself and your industry. Each of these routes is possible, dependent, as we will come to see, on the context of your organization itself and what is possible within your industry as a whole.

Many organizations make decisions on which technologies to invest in more slowly than new technologies that could give them (or others) a competitive advantage become available. This is the natural time and opportunity gap within a traditional business where organizational structures and behaviors dictate that centralized and top-down decisions happen only at the pace that the deliberation and validation of those decisions allow for.

If the lag between leadership decision making and technological advances were to remain the same, that could be manageable but it isn't. As technology evolves exponentially, the gap between organizational change and technological change becomes ever wider. The danger is not just that a business fails to keep pace with customer expectations, but that a new and unforeseen competitor enters your market far higher along the curve of technological change. That entrant is not thinking about investment in technology in the same way as you. For them, the technology and the opportunity it gives them *is* their disruptive business model.

Let me give you an example of where Publicis Sapient helped to prevent that from happening. Some years ago, we were in a conversation with the kind of client that I would describe as a classic change agent. We had worked with him in a number of roles at different companies and now he was working at a large British betting and gambling company. Now, I know gambling is not for everyone, and that it's not a popular industry with some audiences and in some markets. Nevertheless, this company came to us having grown over more than a century but was now threatened by new competitors who were not only better at digital channels but were harnessing technology to create new models, namely peer-to-peer exchange betting.

Our client needed not only to improve its online experience to win back customers, but to go deep into its back-end technology in order to transform the product and service. The solution didn't come from the betting industry at all but from our experience working with financial traders at global investments banks: proprietary technology that made it significantly quicker and easier to set prices, replacing the manual process of odds being calculated by sports experts and providing a much wider range of in-play betting options.

It was the investment in the technology and trading systems that first gave us the opportunity to overlay it with improved online experience, and a new brand and advertising proposition. The excitement of many, many more live betting opportunities became something that was built into the web and mobile experience, with live odds even featuring in the company's TV advertising, something only made possible by the upfront technological investment in its trading platform.

A second challenge that rapid technological progression has presented for traditional businesses is the emergence of entirely new business models based not on the ownership of the means of production, of supply chains, or of inventory, but built almost entirely on the connections that these new technologies have created.

The platform business model – and the technology giants predicated on this model – is one of the greatest business phenomena of the digital age. They are wondrous to behold if you're a neutral observer, rewarding to use if you're a customer or merchant, but troublesome if you operate a business in an industry impacted by one of these unicorns. Whether Amazon or Alibaba, from Airbnb to Uber, and Facebook, Apple, or Google, these platforms have constructed huge communities and exchanges on top of today's connecting technologies.

It's important to note that the platform business model is not the technology itself, but that the technology is what allows the platform to scale quickly and provides for the network effect, the value gained by the user from the rapid addition of users to the benefit of the platform as a whole.

Platform business models and the network effect matter because they disrupt industries and, for established businesses, what they do can be difficult to replicate. The value (and scalability) of an Airbnb or an Uber is that neither, in any real sense, own physical assets while the network grows in size and usefulness every time a new host or driver, guest or rider, signs up. Amazon and Alibaba bring together shoppers and merchants on a vast scale; the larger they get, the more beneficial they become to buyers and sellers, and the more they grow.

Whether you are an international hotel chain or mid-size hotelier facing Airbnb, or a Walmart or an independent retailer facing Amazon, the answer to the challenge presented by these platforms lies within the physical assets, communities, and experiences you uniquely own.

The way to realize those advantages, however, will almost certainly lie with a different and more ambitious mindset toward the technologies that can unlock value for your customers and your business.

It is helpful to think about technological change as a force rather than a thing: a constant business dynamic rather than an end destination. The specific technologies matter, for sure, and all of us would do well to stay abreast of the latest technologies and what they might mean for our businesses and industries. What's more important, though, is to understand the limitations that your organization might have to being able to take up business-critical technologies and, of course, to overcome those limitations.

## Societal Change

At the annual World Economic Forum in Davos, the Business Roundtable – comprising the CEOs of America's leading companies and currently chaired by Walmart CEO Doug McMillon – recently fundamentally started to shift the definition of what a company should be. In a move away from shareholder primacy, the Business Roundtable issued a commitment to lead it's companies for the benefit of all stakeholders: customers, employees, suppliers, communities, and shareholders.

It is certainly the case that the stakeholder group has become a lot more rounded. In the past, companies operated with the sense that "I am the provider of a product or service." Today that is not enough. Customers look at what we do, as well as how we do it, not only in relation to what they touch directly, but across the entire supply chain. They are no longer beholden to a single company, have a wider set of choices, and hold a huge megaphone in terms of being able to influence the perception of a company to millions of other people. The customer, their relationship to the business, and their expectations are different.

I first met Microsoft CEO Satya Nadella in Davos. The theme of that year's World Economic Forum was "Globalization 4.0," which, it turned out, had particular resonance for both of us. For me, the theme was grounded in an understanding that we live and work in an age of transformative change, shaped by technologies that are rapidly and fundamentally altering the way we experience, interact with, and make an impact on the world. Satya has absolute clarity on Microsoft's purpose and intent to make a difference. He understands that technology-driven economic growth must also deliver equitable growth that benefits our communities.

The call for greater oversight of technology giants was (as it is today) a major talking point, and it was interesting to hear Satya's perspective that the right level of pre-emptive regulation can help rather than hinder technology's advance and the material benefits it can bring to people's lives. Older, established businesses – even those in the technology sector – seem to have a more comfortable relationship with the idea of interconnectedness among purpose, value, corporate governance, ethics, and impact on society. There are signs, though, that Satya's prescience in understanding this is now starting to gain broader acceptance among the rest of the technology giants.

## The Role of Purpose

In the age of the customer, a successful organization needs to embody and articulate a clear reason to exist, in line with customer needs. The ability to adapt and transform to the rapid change brought about by digital, in order to remain relevant and protected from competitive risk, is crucial.

As an example, Lego defines its vision as "A global force for establishing and innovating learning-through-play." Lego's mission, separate from its vision, is equally powerful: "Inspire and develop the builders of tomorrow" and is supported by four promises around people, play, partners, and planet.[3] From near bankruptcy in 2004, Lego turned its business around to be named Brand Finance's "Most Powerful Brand in the World" just a decade later. It reframed its business to encompass digital, content, and entertainment, and with renewed purpose delivered record profits. When companies put purpose at the heart of their strategy, they create a bolder vision of sustainable success – financially, socially, and environmentally.

Not coincidentally, those three measures – financial, social, and environmental – are the legs of triple bottom line (TBL) accounting used by so many leading businesses today. Interestingly, John Elkington, the writer who coined the term "triple bottom line" back in 1994, is today working with industry experts to improve upon the TBL system through a new 3Rs framework. Responsibility, Resilience, and Regeneration are the considerations for a digital era, where self-disruption and innovation by businesses and across value chains become an essential part of the new system.[4]

This brings us back to purpose and responsibility, both vital elements to any modern company's sustained success and inextricably linked under the full and inescapable gaze of a digital world.

A company's purpose is so critical because it creates a context for change and at the same time creates a galvanizing connection to drive that change in a seamless way. Purpose is crucial in the midst of any transformation, because often the biggest resistance to change is people not being clear about why they need to change. "Why are we doing this?" "Is this essential?" The company's purpose is what frames the context of what it is trying to achieve. Digital business transformation isn't a destination, it's a journey.

A company's purpose is a higher order question. A "why do we exist?" question. The ability to answer it, instantly and without equivocation, is one of the qualities that characterize a leading digital business. These businesses have laser-like clarity about what they were put on this planet to do. While it could be argued that Silicon Valley firms do stray from their values – think Google and its original code of conduct "Don't Be Evil" – by and large understanding that your purpose is to digitize the world's information creates a driving force for the business to exist beyond its current specific product or service.

**"Be, Say, Do"** The digital world is hugely action oriented, and people within it draw connections between what a company exists to do, what it says, and the actions it takes: the "be, say, and do" of a business. If there is a difference between what you say and what you do, you're going to get called out for it quickly. Purpose is no longer just a mission statement that a company hangs on a wall somewhere. You have to do something about it; that's what makes purpose different in this age versus historically.

Every action that a business takes can now be connected to, or create cognitive dissonance from, its stated purpose. The question every company should be asking itself is how it creates the connection rather than that cognitive dissonance. Your actions are either detracting from the thing you are advocating or you're reinforcing it. As organizations think about transforming, connecting that transformation to their purpose is, essentially, about making purpose core to what they do and not tangential.

The shift, to acknowledge that companies operate in a multistakeholder environment, is widespread. Beyond the company and the customer as the two primary actors in any business relationship, a modern business is more likely to be held accountable for the health of its partner or supply chain network. Beyond that, they are held accountable not just for their own behaviors but for those of the entire ecosystem, which is why child labor or forced labor in the supply chain, among other ethical concerns, carries significant risk for a company and therefore commands so much of its attention.

A further dimension is the responsibility to shareholders: For whom the company's immediate performance and its sustainable business practices are key. In addition, there is now an expectation around a company's product or service and its sustainability more broadly held by customers, shareholders, and a wider group of media and observers. Finally, there is the dimension of society in general and responsibility to people who are outside a company's customer-partner-shareholder ecosystem entirely. When a company aggressively optimizes its tax arrangements, for instance, it runs the risk of damage to reputation and even to revenues, as consumers move to what they regard as more ethical organizations.

Several years ago, before the popularity of the triple bottom line, I was speaking about this connection among purpose, transformation, and value with the CEO of a large, global consumer products company. He had been on a path to connect its strategy more directly to the idea of sustainability. At the time, the company had many products, such as palm oil, that were having an environmental impact. He said, "If I want to have an impact and be more sustainable with our customers, every choice we are making in the business has to be governed this way."

This was well before sustainability became a popular idea and investors and the markets questioned whether this was, in fact, good business. He held strong to his conviction, stating, "I believe sustainability and profitability are not mutually exclusive." The impact of the connection to a greater purpose for the company not only produced environmental and customer benefits, it laid the foundation for his successor, who expanded this legacy to stand up for social causes from changing packaging and marketing that reinforced unhealthy views of skin color in India to support for the Black Lives Matter movement. He also continued to advance the cause of sustainable leadership, talking about border security and the impact on their water supply system and also creating an awards program to generate ideas from young entrepreneurs on how to address the challenges of sustainability more effectively.

As their transformation partner, this clarity of purpose helped us to align our work to the broader impact of their organization and to design products and experiences that advanced those ideals.

Historically, companies might have been measured on the basis of one-to-one relationships with each of those stakeholders. What we see now is that people are taking into account all of these dimensions not just in the context of an investor, customer, or partner; they are starting to be more holistic in their evaluation of a company.

**DBT Takeaway: The Four Forces of Connected Change**

An awareness of the forces of change and the way they are shifting and evolving is important to the understanding of your organization's place in the world – of what it is built to do, the value that it delivers and generates, and how to harness technology to make and keep your product or service relevant.

Later in the book, we will look at the need to align a team around a shared vision as an essential factor in your successful business transformation. Core to that vision, and to the focus on shared outcomes it will elicit, is the ability to unhesitatingly answer questions related to the four forces of connected change:

- In the age of the customer, as power shifts from brands to a growing population of global consumers, how are we designed to identify and incorporate shifting customer expectations in how we create value as they continue to spiral upward?
- How are we structured to evolve with changes in technology that will inevitably come?
- Is our strategy for technology and data one that gives us an improved and connected understanding of customer needs and behaviors, and the ability to serve those customers over time with relevant products and services?
- How do we best utilize our unique combination of physical assets, communities, and experiences to counter incursions by digital, platform-based competitors?
- Can we articulate our purpose in the world, in line with customer needs, and consistently deliver on that promise? Is our reason to exist, and the way we operate our business, in harmony with our stakeholders' expectations of responsible business?

# CHAPTER 3

# What Is Slowing Down Established Businesses?

## Blocks, Brakes, and Behaviors

Have you ever watched Mo Farah run? You've possibly seen the distance runner and four-time Olympic gold medalist win: those moments of elation after the race when, his shoulders draped with a Union Jack flag and the crowd roaring, he performs his trademark "Mobot" celebration by lifting his hands to his head in the shape of an "M." Not that. Have you ever watched Mo Farah actually run?

At the 2012 Olympic Games in London, I was in the fortunate position of being able to take some of our clients to the athletics events on what is now known as "Super Saturday" (the Brits swept up 12 gold medals, so it was "super" for them). On that day, we had trackside seats and, I can tell you, the 10,000 meters final is a long race, even run at Olympian speed. Over the course of 27 minutes and 30.42 seconds you get a lot of time to watch what a champion athlete puts themselves through. It struck me, watching Mo, that mostly it looks like focus, intensity, and pain.

Change can be difficult and it can hurt. You've got to work hard to get in shape, to get from slow to fast, to overcome all those bad habits that are holding you back from optimal performance and to ignore all those niggles, sores, and demons that are telling you it's just too hard.

If you overcome the challenges and put in the hard miles, you will get those fleeting moments of celebration and recognition for all of the work that's been put in. You can look like a winning Mo Farah, but that only comes "after." Success feels good retrospectively.

In order for our companies and organizations to become faster and more agile, we first need to identify what it is that is holding us back. The first thing to understand, to overcome it, is that you were made slow – as an individual and as a business. That may sound harsh, and it's meant to. The only way that we can get from the organizations that we are to the organizations we need to be in a digital world is to identify the blocks, brakes, and behaviors that we perpetuate, and the reasons why we do that.

A good starting point is to recognize that every single thing that has been considered good business practice in the past is largely meaningless in the context of the digital world. Established companies have grown up with an operating assumption that decision making is best done by those people right at the top of the organizational pyramid. It was always better to be slow, considered, and to get as much validation as was possible for key decisions.

These companies were born in a world in which everything was "hard" and hardware behaved in a certain way. In a software world, however, those learned practices need to be unlearned. This is a real challenge because the scale of decision making, the rate of decision making, and the test-and-learn ideas are of an entirely different order from a digital perspective. Your culture, structure, ways of working, and "best practices" are essentially being rewritten.

In my conversations with different clients, at different career stages and levels of management, and across a range of different industries and organization types, the things that are holding them back are remarkably common:

Top-down decision making

Organizational silos

Legacy technology

Short-termism

Talent shortages

Values and culture

"Not invented here"

## Top-down Decision Making

The traditional approach of being linear, deliberative, and constructing a hierarchy of decision making to enable scale is among the most seminal of the blocks to change. Decision making historically has been based on the experience and accumulated expertise of senior leaders. When the methods for creating value were consistent and the pace of change was slower, top-down decision makers had deeper expertise around how decisions could be executed. Today, the process for creating value through digital is iterative across multiple capabilities, and creating the ability to rapidly test and learn is essential. Leaders are faced with not having the relevant expertise in the context of the decisions they need to make.

In addition, the necessary speed of decision making has accelerated and it's likely that your organization is not built to move at that pace. In a traditional business set-up, you might form a hypothesis, do the research, present a business case for funding and make a recommendation, have someone execute that recommendation, and if necessary course correct. This is far removed from the idea of operating in constant beta where not only are you making decisions constantly, but you are constantly updating live products. The need today is to make data-driven decisions, constantly.

Take a building site as an analogy. If you were to take a center-and-up approach, every single contractor involved in constructing the building would need to check with five people before he placed the next brick, or mixed the next batch of cement. It's not agile and could quickly bring things to a halt. That may have been fine in an era when you had 20 years to build that building. Now, if you're trying to build that building in a year or a month, you fundamentally need to shift that approach.

## Organizational Silos

The Chief Digital Officer (CDO) at a leading bank made a comment that has always stayed with me, "The greatest impact I can have in this organization is helping them realize that if the individual capabilities within our business units don't work together, we'll never be able to scale to do something transformational and will only ever be able to make incremental change." It was a profound insight, and showed an incredible clarity of purpose.

The reality, though, was the silos that existed within the organization were deeply entrenched. Instead of achieving that goal, the company decided to instead invest within business units instead of connecting across. The CDO? Well, he left the company shortly after. His experience highlights the reality of this particular challenge. Even with the best-laid plans and visions, silos are not just about structure; they require getting people to operate very differently.

Organizational silos were built in and for a world that was reasonably linear: "We're going to start manufacturing a product, then we're going to market it, and then we're going to sell it." There was a certain sequence, resembling a factory assembly line, which meant that you didn't, for instance, have to worry about marketing until after the product was built. Similarly, you didn't need to pay too much attention to customer feedback until the next product cycle.

Many established businesses have not felt the need to evolve that model since the industrial age. They had not felt the need to collaborate more and certainly not to collaborate in a more iterative fashion. If you wanted funding for a project, the budgets were established up front in a business plan, a year or two in advance. Then you went about making the product, and when the product was approaching completion you might market that product. Then you got your sales force involved in selling it, after which you would train your retail or call center operations to deal with the support for that product. Eventually, you would use some of that customer feedback iterating on the next generation of the product. But what happens where you go from a "hard" world to "soft," and every one of these things is happening in a real-time cycle as opposed to a day, let alone a week or month, and every one of those previously linear stages has to be acted upon at once and in real time?

What's interesting about organizational silos is that, in the past, silos and hierarchy were a key ingredient to how companies could scale their business. You needed the structure to serve a broader client base or expand into new markets. While the quest for scale is still important, the means to scale must evolve and embrace networks rather than hierarchies.

Historically, business functions could operate largely independently of each other. Marketing, for instance, had no role in the context of a customer complaint. What's changed is that now a customer might Tweet if they are in a city and can't seem to get a hotel room at their preferred brand. As a consequence, that brand's marketing team and pricing people have to talk to the hotel operation management function. The three of them have to determine if they're going to respond, and who's going to respond. Silos get in the way of collaborative solutions as, by definition, they were never designed for it.

Not only is the function of marketing changing, because now it is disintermediated by technology and data, but how marketing affects customer service is also changing. So people are having to accept and adapt to change in and of their own function, as well as to change in the way that they interact with other functions. How successful businesses are at that fundamentally comes down to personality, agendas, and our ability to learn, unlearn, and relearn. People's drivers, their agendas, and their ability to process information are all a factor in how successful an organization will be at transforming.

How quickly a single person can process information is one of the great limitations of decision making today. A general on a historic battlefield would run infantry and cavalry, and had very simple data points to infer from. Information was reaching him from human beings within those units who would report back to him by radio. Today, a military commander is dealing with satellite overlay, drone feedback, real-time impact assessments on tanks and vehicles in battle, and information from the soldiers' biometrics and body cams. What is the capacity of a person to be able to make good decisions in this context?

A large part of digital business transformation in organizations is to help more people make fewer, better decisions that only they are suited to make and to try to get as many decisions as they don't need to make taken off them at a senior level and pushed down lower into the organization. We also seek to augment these people with decision-making tools that simplify the decision for them, or that present the information to them in a way that makes the decision easier by synthesizing lots of different kinds of information.

One thing that happens in complex environments of high change is that you typically see certain behaviors. The first is psychological safety, where you retreat back to what you know is going to create safety for you and your organization. You might try to oversimplify, to minimize, or talk down the change i.e., to deny that much change is coming. The second is that you decide your primary focus is to protect the interests of your team or yourself. By and large, people understand the need for change, but one of the things organizations struggle with is communication. Often, not everyone in the organization is bought into the fact that change is needed. And even if they are, they are certainly not bought into the idea that this is the actual change that is needed.

We all see examples, all the time, of organizational silos and divisional interests operating against the best interests of the companies we work for or with. They are prevalent and certainly are not unique to your experience or business. Take a retail client that we partnered with on their transformation: there are many people who continue to believe that fundamentally the business is doing fine and that what they're going through is just a phase. The people who are responsible for the large physical outlets continue to have an orientation of minimizing the change entirely: that the digital business is all well and good but it doesn't actually affect what they have got to do.

## Legacy Technology

"Legacy," in the context of technology, is a polite way of saying "out of date." Few business leaders are willing to acknowledge that something that is so critical to that company's success is no longer fit for purpose. That's understandable. It's because these systems are so business-critical that they don't get replaced: They are big, complex, and the cost as well as the risk of replacing them leads to a crucial investment decision being deferred. This is a key reason why a company's once shiny new technology investments become "legacy." An increasingly hazardous cycle of cladding or bolting new additions on to an already creaking systems structure ensues.

To many people, the word digital in the context of their business has implied the advertising or marketing technology stack. In a consumer goods company, for example, they may ask "what does a manufacturing system have to do with digital?" and come up with the answer "not much", at least in theory. If you're in a bank, "digital" is taken to mean your website and your mobile app i.e., all of the front end of your architecture.

Typically, the front end is imagined to be digital. In a world that is entirely about a business being digital, there is no such thing as a front end or middleware as distinct from your back end, which is often where your mainframe and real legacy technologies live. All that matters is getting the service to the customer. Even if you have a very fast, modern, evolving front end, it is reliant on big legacy technologies. Legacy technology presents a huge challenge because it breaks down the end-to-end process.

Historically, technology was about risk and cost, to the extent that the technology felt as though it was going to prevent an imminent risk. The other balance companies always had to maintain was keeping costs low. If the only purpose of technology was to minimize risk, pairing risk up with cost made a lot of sense. It was an approach where IT creates a risk and a cost and reports to the CFO versus an approach where technology is about being able to create real differentiation and value – value to the customer and differentiation around the product and service. Through that lens, technology is not the thing that is ancillary to the service but it *is* the service.

The risk and cost approach is a "house of cards" approach to technology. What risk and cost oriented companies tend to do is to paper over the messy, spaghetti code of back-end systems with something that barely allows you to interface with those systems. The mindset is that the risk and cost are too high. In fact, the rate of change and cost of change are inversely proportionate to the amount of change you make. The more changes you make to papering over the spaghetti, the more money it costs you and the longer it takes. The more you keep doing that the more you perpetuate your problem until the entire system falls over.

Part of the reason that technologies evolve in different places and at different rates within a business is that budgetary responsibility for the technology is also siloed. The CMO needed marketing technology, which meant the CIO was expected to deliver the technology to support marketing: that's one silo. The chief customer services officer, meanwhile, expected the CIO to deliver all the technology to support customer services: another silo. As these systems start to become more iterative and interdependent, those ways of working mean you need greater consensus in terms of driving change through technology. In turn this falls back to human behavioral barriers. Whose budget pays for this; is it mine or yours? Where the entire business is digital, these technology silos tend not to exist.

## Short-termism

Amazon famously spends more than $16 billion on research and development, reinvests revenue into future growth, and is relatively relaxed about how quickly its investments turn a profit. That's all very well for Amazon; its shareholders give the company financial leverage and time that established organizations are rarely afforded. Many CEOs have shared with me their frustrations that they could easily transform their business if only they didn't have to worry about the short-term performance of their business and the next quarter's financials.

The focus of many established companies, both private and public, is on this quarterly earnings cycle. A consequence can be the avoidance of risk, the need to show ongoing and growing profits, to maintain PE ratios and EBITDA performance, and to deliver dividends accompanied by high share prices. All of this is the antithesis of investing for growth, and causes leaders too often to make the risk-averse, safest, and worst investment decisions.

Similarly, an established business is likely to take a present-state approach to investment, and choose not to invest if the numbers suggest that the return will not have a significant impact on revenue and profitability. This approach falls into the trap of considering the present cost of investing, while ignoring the future, stored-up costs of not investing, the effect of which can compound over time. As we have seen, people are not the best at recognizing the scale and speed of change, or the real risk of disruption to their business or industry.

An established company operating with a present-state approach can, therefore, take a series of "non-investment" decisions, the consequences of which may not become apparent for some time but which ultimately jeopardize its future in a digital age.

## Talent Shortages

You don't have to look far to see the rising talent challenges faced by companies, governments, and institutions across the world. The World Economic Forum has estimated that at least 133 million new technology roles will have been generated globally between 2018 and 2022 and that 54% of all employees will require significant reskilling and upskilling.[1] Meanwhile, global organizational consulting and talent firm Korn Ferry estimates that, by 2030, the technology sector alone will have a skills shortage of 4.3 million workers.[2]

An optimist may say that's an indicator of incredible growth and opportunity. And it is. But, for companies in the process of becoming digital themselves, it's incredibly daunting. While 90% of maturing companies expect digital disruption, only 44% are adequately preparing for it.[3]

Some of the areas where established companies are seeing the most significant skills gaps are in AI and data science, where there simply aren't enough experienced people to meet the demand for what are, and will be, vital elements of companies' potential to identify and realize future customer value.

What options are available to business leaders and hiring managers at established companies? The ability to attract and retain the best digital and engineering talent is a twofold challenge for them.

First, they are in competition with leading digital businesses which may already have strong cultures, capabilities, and ways of working and are therefore attractive employers for talent entering the workforce. The conundrum for established businesses is how to attract talent whose inclination may be to join a digitally native company where the technology capability and "constant beta" approach is already established.

Second, the technology skills that we need in our organizations are changing rapidly, and the risk is investing in the wrong kind of talent, or that even if you invest in the right talent, you are unable to retain them. And, let's face it, replacing talent is incredibly costly. Turnover costs for highly skilled positions can be 213% of salary.[4]

The solutions available are limited, and not without their own challenges. Of course, it's possible to pay above the market rate to attract the talent with the necessary skills, assuming you can find them. The likely immediate difficulty here is that the skills and experience needed are changing all the time and within a few years those expensive new hires will have skills shortages of their own.

The answer lies with continually reskilling and upskilling your existing talent. Curiously, given the importance and potential impact of addressing the technology skills gap, many businesses are being slow to respond. It all comes back to the short-term behaviors that run through this chapter. Too often, our choices are driven by the more immediate concerns: is budget available, and when will our key technology people possibly have the spare time to complete training?

It's important to recognize that choices driven by the short-term challenges, however legitimate they may be at the time, are the blocks and brakes that slow you down. Conversely, those companies that make a priority of future-proofing their people by implementing continual reskilling and a culture of learning and development, will be those best equipped to prosper as they navigate change.

## Values and Culture (and Purpose)

Management thinking generally has it that a company with a distinct, deep, and unifying culture and values is a strong company. While that is true, it is only beneficial if "strong" does not, in practice, look more like "rigid" and "unyielding."

A company's culture and values are often a reflection of its origins, provenance, and founders. Even where those characteristics and characters existed centuries ago, the culture and values of an established business are often championed by and best embodied by the leaders of the company, and by those employees who have been with the organization the longest (which are often the same thing). Again, a culture and values that run deeply through an organization can be one of its greatest strengths, and no one assigns much worth to a culture or values that change every year.

The risk to established companies comes where its culture and values become blockers to change: to identifying new opportunities or embracing new processes. The culture and values that are defined and lived by a tight-knit group of executives can manifest themselves as entrenched thinking and methods, which generate the greatest of brakes on transformative change.

We'll look in greater detail at the behaviors and characteristics of a successful digital organization later in this book, but for now we need to identify and guard against company cultures and values that become excuses for not doing something rather than the enablers of new ideas and approaches. If you think that your organization is more prone to the former, then it may pay to focus more on purpose than culture and values. A successful organization today needs to embody a clear reason to exist, in line with customer needs. The ability to adapt and transform to the rapid change brought about by digital, in order to remain relevant and protected from competitive risk, is crucial.

## "Not Invented Here"

Orthodoxy is an obstacle, a great, muscular beast of an obstacle that will almost always stand obstinately between you and whatever it is you want to change. Why? Because whatever it is that you are trying to progress, by definition, represents a challenge to that orthodoxy, which is a threat to existing systems, power structures, beliefs, methods, or behaviors.

The more successful a company has historically been, the bigger it becomes and, often, the more inclined it is to try to mirror and repeat whatever is was that made it successful in the first place. When a strong, but unrecognizable, idea comes along, the inclination for an established organization is to test it against entrenched behaviors, risk, cost, and perceived reward.

The end result is that historically successful companies are at the greatest risk of losing what it is that made them successful in the first place. They weren't born complacent, arrogant or slow-footed. It is their market leadership and the pressure to sustain short-term growth in revenue and profit that leads them to spurn non-orthodox opportunities. This differs from the approach that a digital entrant might take, where new ideas are more readily embraced and experimented with until another strong idea comes along that improves upon what went before.

### DBT Takeaway: What Is Slowing Your Business Down?

There are some common themes that surface with clients around what is slowing down established businesses. In order to transform, leaders need to be aware of these often intangible blockers: the choices, agendas, and resistance to change that can come between them and their ability to create digital organizations.

Successful digital business transformation requires that you anchor in outcomes. Established businesses are often challenged by knowing what to let go of and what to keep, which is where clarity on business outcomes is crucial. Being able to identify and address the blocks, brakes, and behaviors is far easier when viewed through the lens of business outcomes – helping to avoid the trap of attachment to past bad habits, or to check off deliverables and outputs without ever achieving the outcomes.

The reason that 70% of digital transformations fail is to be found in the most common blocks, brakes, and behaviors:

- *Top-down decision making*. Many established businesses are hardwired for top-down decision making, which directly conflicts with their ability to evolve at pace with the changes around them.
- *Organizational silos*. Today's customer experiences require much tighter coordination between front-end and back-end processes. Most organizations are built with an emphasis on distinct areas of expertise versus the collaboration across them.
- *Legacy technology*. Technical debt built over decades creates a unique challenge for established companies, which have to navigate existing technology investment and reconcile that with the need for agility in their engineering capability.
- *Short-termism*. When we're faced with an investment decision, where the choice is between setting up something entirely new at considerable cost or to leverage something that already exists and where the cost is marginal, it is the latter that will almost always win out. This limits the opportunity to really address digital business transformation and produce the outcomes that are possible.
- *Talent shortages*. Established businesses are losing out to digitally native companies on talent, especially engineering talent. In addition, the pace of technological change can paralyze investment in future talent needs.

- *Values and culture.* The culture and values that are defined and lived by a tight-knit group of executives can manifest themselves as entrenched thinking and methods, which generate the greatest of brakes on transformative change.
- *"Not invented here."* Adoption of new ways of working are often challenged by the entrenched, established norms that made the company successful to begin with.

# SECTION 2

# NEXT

# CHAPTER 4

# Characteristics of a Digital Business

*"When digital transformation is done right, it's like a caterpillar turning into a butterfly. But when done wrong, all you have is a really fast caterpillar."*

– George Westerman, MIT Sloan Initiative on the Digital Economy. © 2017, SLOAN SCHOOL OF MANAGEMENT.

## The Inconvenient Truth

The CEO of a major retailer was telling me recently about one of the things he does regularly to make sure that his business is properly serving its customers' needs. He started working at the company when he was 19 years old, stacking shelves, and today runs what is one of the largest retail businesses in the world. It's a great business, and much of that is down to the actions of a CEO and leadership team that care deeply about the company and its customers.

"I walk through the stores and I watch people. I watch our customers. I watch what they do, I watch how they buy, I watch how they engage with products, I watch which aisles they walk through, I watch where they spend time. I talk to them. I understand what they like and what they don't like."

That is the perfect model for what it takes to be a good retailer: be with your customers and understand them.

However, to him, that idea of spending time in his stores and getting close to his customers was very different from looking at a screen to observe and understand the very same things. In his lifetime as CEO, the online channel had become his biggest store and it held the key to understanding whether people are clicking on the top left-hand navigation to shop or using the search function to find products, and whether they were dropping out at certain points in the checkout and abandoning their shopping baskets. He didn't quite appreciate that the store visits and web analytics were essentially the same thing. He understood it conceptually, of course, but the good digital practice was not in his DNA. What was true for him is true for a lot of established, or pre-digital, companies.

The inconvenient truth is that most companies are great at their core business, but not great at reimagining the future of their business. In a world where much of what we do and know has gone digital in the space of an average CEO's career, and the rest of it is not far behind, established businesses need help. They need help to balance the pressure to perform in their current context with the need to transform in the context of a digital world.

How many businesses that we work for or with today may not survive, let alone thrive, a few years from now? All you have to do is pick up a copy of *The Wall Street Journal* and see stock prices in decline, falling growth rates, shrinking margins, meaning businesses in trouble. Many of the top companies of yesterday have been overtaken by those that were born digital or that have digital at their core. Figure 4.1 shows a comparison of the top five US companies by market capitalization in 2001 and today.

The chart makes stark reading, but there is a bright spot. At the time that those companies in the left-hand column were top of the pile, digital was a tangential idea. The CEO of a major retail company might have told you that he had an ecommerce manager, because ecommerce was something interesting happening over there, as an adjunct to the main business. Talk to a retail CEO today and the only

| 2001 | Market cap (bn) |
|---|---|
| General Electric | $406 |
| Microsoft | $365 |
| Exxon | $272 |
| Citicorp | $261 |
| Walmart | $260 |

| 2020 | Market cap (bn) |
|---|---|
| Microsoft | $1328 |
| Apple | $1238 |
| Amazon | $1201 |
| Alphabet (Google) | $879 |
| Facebook | $542 |

**FIGURE 4.1** Today's top five US companies by market cap (as of April 24, 2020) compared with those of 2001

kind of commerce he's talking about is the one that's happening digitally, because it's happening everywhere: in his stores, online, and on mobile devices. The same is true of nearly every company of size in every sector. In board rooms around the world, business leaders are discussing the need for digital transformation as the means to identify and unlock exponential value by driving growth, increasing efficiency, and creating better experiences for customers.

Let's nail our colors to the mast. Would it not be a disaster if the only retailer in the world were Amazon because they were the only company to figure out how to sell us everything? And if the only social community in the world were Facebook? Who wants to be in a place like that? As much as we want start-ups to fly and for digital entrants to improve and redefine products and experiences, we also want those brands that we grew up with, those we appreciate and trust, to succeed by evolving to be relevant in the world today for us, and for the generations to come.

The challenge, then, is not to just recognize the imperative for transformation. We have passed that milestone and will not be returning to it. The challenge is to develop the vision as well as the road map to get there; to identify opportunities for disruption, but also to understand how you will go about delivering it; to identify and remove the obstacles to transformation that exist within your business, while replacing them with the qualities and behaviors of a digital-at-the-core organization.

## Decoding What Digital Companies Do Well

I once had a date with Tinder. Not a date *using* Tinder, you understand. I'm just on the wrong side of that generation. I met up with Sean Rad, the founder of Tinder, at the annual Cannes festival of creativity. On a few different levels, he and I had a connection.

I'm a huge fan of solving things in the human experience that we didn't know we needed. In the realm of online dating, there was too much information on too many people when what the target demographic was used to was speed. The interaction design of Tinder is to scroll and swipe, an experience optimized for modern dating. Sean is happy to relate how Tinder invented the "swipe" as a decision maker, which has gone on to be copied as a gestural standard across many different businesses and industries operating in a fast-paced world.

Not all of them though. It's surprising how many businesses fail to get this right – from retailers' online checkout to airlines' boarding pass downloads. It's extraordinary, when you consider that the interaction could be the reason a customer picks you over someone else – that an established organization struggles to put the same emphasis on this aspect of experience as a digital native does – almost instinctively.

There's much more that Tinder got right: being clear that its purpose is to solve a universal problem about meeting people, the emphasis on slick and speedy experience, and the central idea that the extraordinary amount of data input via the app is the fuel to evolve and improve the product and its value in customers' lives.

Tinder is a useful reference to consider as we start to decode what it is that makes the most successful digital businesses today and identify the qualities that they share in common. Established businesses, on the other hand, find doing the same things very difficult in their current context and in opposition to their existing structural, operational, and behavioral constraints.

Figure 4.2 shows six things that leading digital businesses consistently do very well. The first quality that they share is to have a very clear idea of what need they are serving or what problem they are

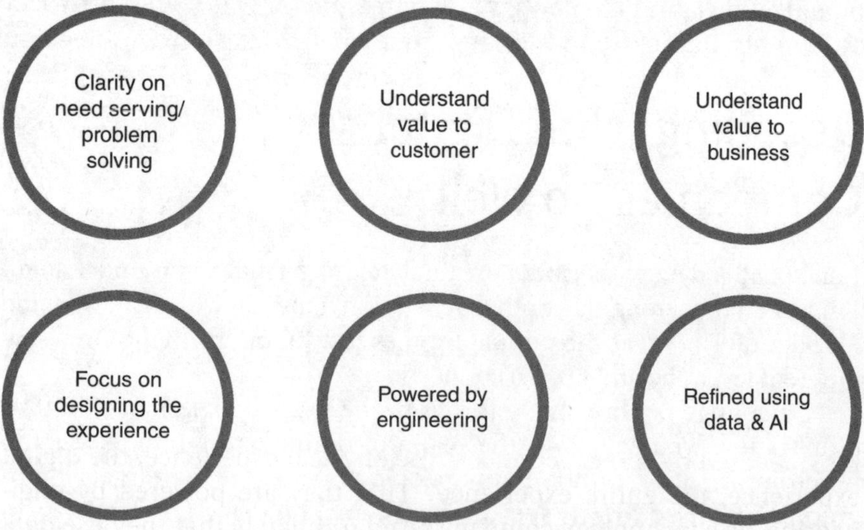


**FIGURE 4.2** Shared qualities of leading digital businesses

solving, and for whom. You wouldn't find a single start up today that couldn't tell you these things within a couple of very concise sentences. The reason that clarity is so powerful is because it allows them to focus. It allows them to be the thing that they were born to be.

Digital businesses are also very quick to understand the value to the customer of what they do. They are very clear on what the benefit of their product or service is to the user. They also understand the value to their business. A digital business will quickly go from "we are creating this much value for the customer" to "here is the value to us in our business and here is how we can be valued."

Leading digital businesses focus on designing the experience. They understand that there is a direct link among value to the customer, value to the business, and quality of the experience and they are applying data, AI, and machine learning to keep pace with changes in customer expectations and needs.

They are powered by engineering. They understand that if you're a bank you are in fact a software company. If you're a retailer, you're a software company. If you're a healthcare provider, you're a software company. That is because, when engineering and technology are core to how ideas are conceived, all of these businesses are intrinsically able to turn them into reality.

Even more important than that, their engineering capability and mindset provide them with the final quality of a leading digital business: the ability to continually refine themselves using their data and inputs. Rather than thinking about whether or not they are going to be a company that is in the same business it was in yesterday, these companies are constantly looking at the inputs they gain from customers and using that data to refine and evolve their business.

This all seems very easy, right? If we put these six steps in front of the leaders of companies large and small, and from a variety of industries, they will say, "That's right, we agree, these are the criteria for success." But how many businesses do we know, that we work with or for, that are truly able to say they are doing what they were born to do, that they have that kind of focus and driving clarity of vision? And that they understand their value to the customer, and consequently understand that value to the business? And that they are first and foremost focused on the experience – the physical experience, the digital experience, the entire experience? That they are powered by engineering, as a technology company? And ultimately that they use data and AI not for reporting, not for looking at historical performance, but to constantly evolve their business because that's where you identify those adjacent opportunities, those areas of growth where you see businesses that started in one place but morphed into another in order to be successful.

## Decoding How They Do It

If we take the idea that your digital moat is the capability that fuels your competitiveness in a digital world, the next logical question is: so how do you build a digital moat? First, let's be clear on what you are designing for: You are building a company that can drive business outcomes through its ability to evolve products, services, and experiences in sync with changing customer behavior and technology.

When we talk about transforming businesses, our aim is to shift our companies or organizations significantly from where they are today and to build in the capabilities and behaviors the leading digital businesses execute exceptionally well. That's not a quick fix. It is not enough just to improve the customer or user experience, and, even if it were, making a substantive improvement to the experience will likely require some fundamental changes to the whole of the business.

To effectively transform a business, leaders need to look at their business model as a whole as Figure 4.3 illustrates. Even one seemingly small improvement in user experience can require changes across multiple levels of an enterprise.

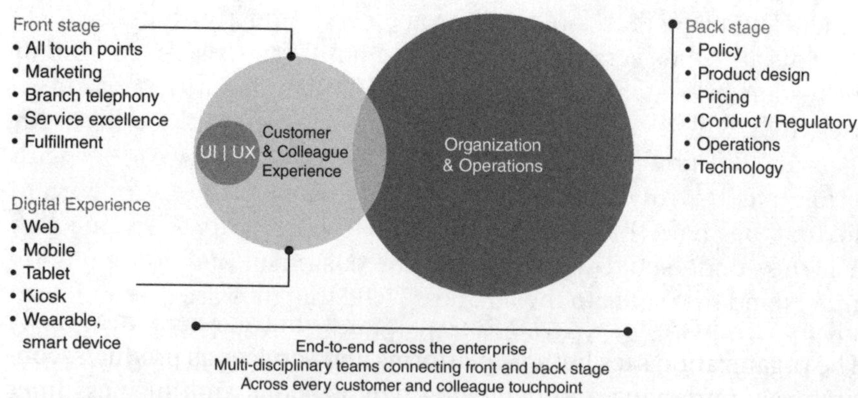


**FIGURE 4.3** End-to-end transformation

That user experience, the simple thing that it is easiest to see, is important, but so too is the experience that surrounds that: the broader experience. How does the shopping app or banking or healthcare app connect to the store, the branch, the doctor's surgery? How does it actually get products delivered? How does it connect to that broader experience? And from there, it's right that we want to transform the user experience and that we recognize that the user experience is connected to that broader experience, but how, then, do we think about product and policy, people, operations, and technology?

Consider the digital enablement of a typical drive-through restaurant. The benefits are evident: a mobile platform would reduce costs, increase revenue, and benefit visitors' overall experience. It would make "fast" food even faster. In order to deliver that improved experience, however, the business needs to look deep and wide at the other aspects of its operations that must be transformed in parallel; all of a sudden, the fast-food chain would need to be aware of exactly which car each customer was arriving in and when, not to mention the amount of in-kitchen and parking processes that need altering and adopting.

By widening our lens of transformation to include multiple facets of the business, it becomes easier to identify a point of untapped expectation within the customer journey and use that to illuminate a path of transformation across the whole enterprise.

Gone are the days when transformation efforts could be molded into a project mindset, with a clear beginning and end, justified solely by typical measurements of cost, time, and scope. The true potential of transformation today lies in value, differentiation, and productivity: three metrics representing a strategic shift in mindset from project to *product*.

A product improves constantly in an effort to serve consumers' wants and needs. Some updates require retiring parts of the product, while others result in a complete revamp from one version to the next. Either way, each update (no matter how big or small, revolutionary or incremental) is an evolution.

Amazon is a good example of a company that does this well. Each step in the brand's evolution has marked a significant iteration and disruption of its own business, technologies, processes, and people, all the while remaining an evolutionary journey of their core idea. How? The organization sees both its platforms and services as products, continuously improving and deploying new versions and business lines by using data in ways other companies have yet to consider. This approach – a combination of data aggregator and disruptor – is what allows the brand to inject itself into people's lives in a way that consistently eases wants and satisfies desires.

Often when we think of an experience, a product, or service, what we start to think about is the part that we see as consumers. One analogy is an iceberg, where the experience is the part that sits above the waterline and is visible to everyone. Figure 4.4 illustrates the factors in play when a retailer considers its ecommerce experience: not just what the customers sees but everything within the business that impacts the experience. For Amazon, the experience might be Prime Now, and it means my product is delivered to me within a couple of hours. If you think through, this not as a consumer but from a business perspective; it introduces significant complexity to operations from a scale and agility perspective and changes to logistics and the supply chain in order to deliver on this promise. You see, even for Amazon, it's not easy.

For other, more established companies than Amazon, this voluntary disruption in order to evolve their business is an even harder concept to understand and to implement. Now, many people might say, "Wouldn't it be cool if General Motors could just become Lyft?"

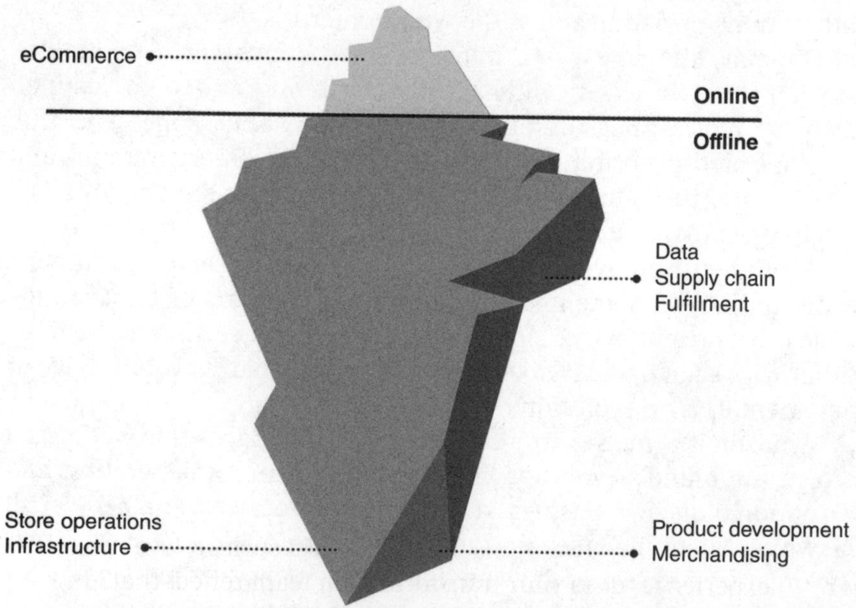


**FIGURE 4.4** Factors impacting the "experience" of ecommerce in retail

The automotive giant bought a significant stake in the ride-sharing service in 2016. Lyft is the app and it is the experience; it's the part of the iceberg people see. Underneath the water, however, is everything else that GM would have to transform along the way. This is not how those established companies have tended to think about their business. They don't think about a customer journey that cuts across user experience, the broader experience, and their organization and operations in a single slice and then ask, "How can we reinvent (to reflect) that?" That's not how they were built, although that has begun to change.

### DBT Takeaway: Characteristics of a Digital Business

The inconvenient truth is that most companies are great at their core business but not great at reimagining the future of their business. This is a challenge for established business but rarely trips up leading digital businesses, where the things they do well are all pointing in the same direction: to be an organization that can change at the pace of change that surrounds it and is able to identify and realize value for its customers and business.

This book sets out to guide you to successful business transformation and often that can involve thinking, acting, and building like a start-up. Easy to say, harder to do. Your organization can't copycat what digital businesses do well, because you're not digitally native. What you can do is to consider those characteristics of a digital business and use your unique combination of assets and skills to transform within the frame of those characteristics:

- Is the core team, and crucially the C-level team, aligned behind a crystal clear vision of their purpose in the world? That's not the same as knowing what the business does, or has always done. Rather, it is clarity on what need you are serving, what problem you are solving, and for whom.
- Does that team have a shared understanding of your organization's value to the customer, and consequently understand that value to the business?
- If experience is everything that impacts on a customer's interactions with your business, not just surface-level user experience, does your transformation team reflect that? Is it multidisciplinary, covering everything from product and policy, to people, operations, and technology?

- Is everything that you are and do underpinned by an engineering capability and mindset? Your goal is to become a technology company, regardless of the industry you operate in. A great engineering capability will allow you to move fast, across different product or service lines, and bring relevant products to market much faster.
- How will you properly use data and AI to constantly evolve and refine your business, in line with where the feedback and inputs from your existing products and services are telling you to go next?

# CHAPTER 5

# The Big Hairy Audacious Goals (BHAGs) of Digital Business Transformation

When leaders of established businesses reach out about digitally transforming their companies, they know they need to do something differently. Sometimes, they are on the receiving end of disruption of their business model, other times they see the potential of digital for their business and want to explore what's possible, or, in some cases, they see changing technology or customer behavior and want to understand the implications. They're often searching for answers to a whole host of questions: How do you make the leap forward into digital while taking your teams with you? Where do you begin? For those who have already started, where do you go next?

The first step is to be very clear about the goals of any digital business transformation. The reality is that teams are made up of people who process information differently. Whether you're a plant manager or a CEO, you've probably been part of a project where you start with an objective that slowly morphs over time. I'm not talking about the situations where an insight shifted your direction. I'm talking about those common everyday moments when well-meaning team members veer off course and lose the plot on what you were setting out to accomplish to begin with. The intention isn't bad; it's just that somewhere along the way they lost sight of the objective.

Where companies often lose their way is when they make bets on a capability, acquire a company, or even launch an innovative new product without connecting those choices back to two fundamental ideas. Without the tie back to these larger outcomes, companies never realize the potential these investments were intended to make, but, more importantly, they never realize their own digital potential. This is why it's important that leaders are able to clearly articulate what's the point of digital business transformation, anyway?

## The Two BHAGs of Digital Business Transformation

Ultimately, digital business transformation is aimed at driving two outcomes:

1. Creating an organization that can continually change at pace with the changes around it
2. Constructing the capability to identify and realize value through digital for your customers and business

Every action, large or small, should ladder up to these two ideas while supporting the specific vision and outcomes you have for your organization. And these two outcomes are not mutually exclusive. It's in their combination where you create something really powerful.

In their book *Competing Against Time,* authors George Stalk and Thomas Hout introduced the idea of time as the most powerful source of competitive advantage.[1] In a world that is rapidly evolving, the idea of managing time as a strategic asset and creating the systems and ways of working to accelerate responsiveness, adaptability, and speed to market is incredibly relevant. In fact, this concept is so important that Tim Cook recommends this book to every Apple new hire.

What the two BHAGs allow you to do is create a simple frame to test whether the transformation activities you're undertaking are actually increasing your ability to evolve and innovate with speed.

## Goal 1: Developing the Muscle of Continuous Change (the PS How)

How you approach your transformation is your first opportunity to start to embed, into the way you operate at every level, the idea of creating an organization that can continuously change. Now you may be thinking, "Yes, of course, we always opt to incorporate agile in our transformation programs." I'd argue you need to take that one step further and actually look at how your business(es) operate in this construct.

One of the common pitfalls we see with clients is they map out a compelling vision, set of outcomes, and road map for their transformation, but then go about the governance and execution of it using the same waterfall approach to project-based work and change management processes of the past. It's easy to see how this happens. Your entire organization is wired to work in this way. The problem is, while it feels more familiar and easier to navigate, it jeopardizes one of the fundamental outcomes we just mentioned: creating an organization that can continuously change. That's a huge outcome to risk!

As we were seeing these challenges creep up more and more with clients, we wanted a way for them to very simply set their transformation activities in the context of both navigating change and creating value. So, the expectations of "done" were no longer about whether a system was integrated or solution was implemented, but whether it was done while feeding back into a continuous loop of value creation.

We created the Publicis Sapient How (PS How) as that overarching frame – see Figure 5.1. The Publicis Sapient How lays out how value is identified and realized continuously in a digital business. It has five activities that can happen concurrently: Ignite, Hunt, Shape, Incubate, and Build & Scale. Depending on where you are in your journey, you could come in at any of these points. For the sake of simplicity, we will take them in order.

The first set of activities centers on Ignite. This is where you are making the case for digital business transformation and looking to gain stakeholder support. Often times what kicks off this part of the life

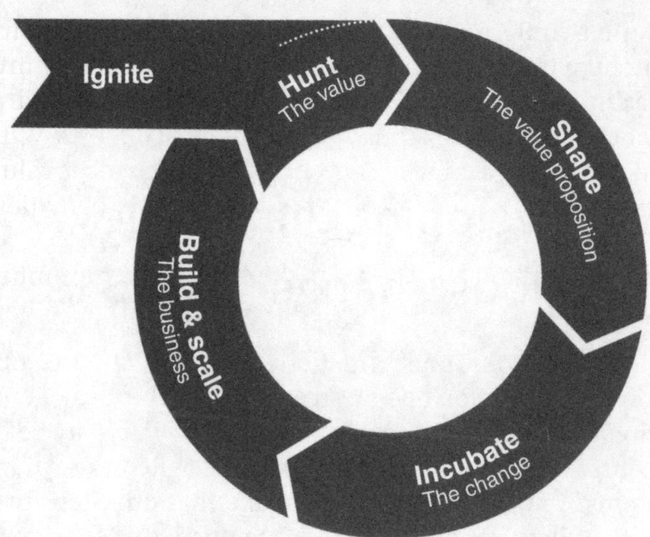


**FIGURE 5.1** The Publicis Sapient "How" frame

cycle is a client asking questions like: Why is transformation necessary? How have technology and changing customer behaviors impacted my industry? What do I need to change in my own business? If you think back to classical consulting, this is often where strategy plays a big role in shaping the vision, market context, and paths forward.

The next activity is Hunt. The Hunt activities are where you identify the potential customer and business value pools you could pursue. This is where you dig into how customer needs are evolving and how that influences "where to play" and "how to win." Identifying those needs is how you'll find potential customer and business value pools that can be further refined and executed upon. The biggest change we've seen in recent years is clients saying "don't tell me what I can do", show me. As a result, prototypes are playing an increasing role in both visualizing what's possible and helping stakeholders come along on the journey. Even if you start with a rapid prototype, what this activity does is validate whether that initial hypothesis still holds and helps you create a road map to move forward. Later in the book, we will dig into this more. The reality for most businesses is Hunt will not just produce one set of activities. It will create a portfolio of moves that will need to be prioritized and coordinated.

The Shape activities are where that prioritization happens. This is done by creating testable hypotheses for each value pool and then using data, research, feedback, modeling, and analysis techniques to refine your hypothesis and probe the consequences of your investment choices. This will give you a clearer sense of the scale and potential impact of business, organizational, and technical change. With that in mind, you can weigh which areas will produce the most value, where (and when) to focus your energy, and validate the activities against your desired outcomes.

Incubate is exactly that: where you can create Minimum Viable Products (MVPs) and test their viability in the market. Where prototypes give you a starting point, this is where pilots can be leveraged to see how audiences react. It will also be where you can start testing product-market fit: is this meeting the needs of customers? Who is the primary audience? How much monetary potential is there (whether in revenue or cost)?

Last is Build & Scale. The MVPs that were piloted are now scaled to the desired audience(s). As we saw in previous chapters, once a product or service is at the point of Build & Scale, the capabilities that it includes will continue to optimize it. What the SPEED capabilities do is create that perpetually evolving system that feeds into this life cycle so Build & Scale doesn't become the final stop, but just another set of activities that feed back into the continuous Hunt for value. By setting your transformation in this frame, you can start to build the muscle within your organization to operate in a state of constant change.

## Goal 2: Building the Capability to Identify and Realize Value (SPEED)

That brings us to our second outcome: constructing the capability to identify and realize value through digital. Remember, we are long past the days where digital meant technology that operated tangentially to the rest of the business.

Think about auto manufacturers. Over the years, the idea of the value people get from their cars has completely changed. For decades, cars were all about their hardware: the literal nuts and bolts of their physical design. Today's cars are as much about software as they are hardware. How does my car connect to the rest of my life? How is it designed to capture my habits and needs? And then, how does the data coming back from the car factor into an iterative design of the car itself? If you think about the dealership model, cars can now be delivered like groceries. In that environment, how are dealerships and inventory relevant? These dynamics are not some tangential options that manufacturers can opt in or out of; they are fundamental to how this industry is evolving. Is there an auto manufacturer in the world who doesn't think mobility and the rise of Uber and Lyft will have an impact on its business? None that we've seen.

As a result, our conversations with CEOs are increasingly centered on how their companies transform how and where value is created. What's interesting is one who shared that, "I don't think our business understands the economic value creation engine of the company and how we make money. The majority of the money we make doesn't actually come from selling new cars." For people not in the auto industry, this may seem counterintuitive. However, it's true in the traditional sense of the business and also creates opportunity for what's possible.

We were speaking about the idea of cars as platforms and talked about this idea in relation to Apple and the iPhone. If iPhone sales were the primary driver of revenue, Apple would have faced a similar challenge to these auto manufacturers: There would be a limited number of revenue streams to sustain the business. By creating a platform where developers could launch new apps and expanding from there, Apple created a much wider digital moat around its business.

Our conversation shifted to thinking about the car as a platform. He observed, "We are so far away from thinking about services because the entirety of the business thinks of itself as building a product. So our partners are seen as clients and not actual partners because they're all viewed in relation to the disparate parts of the business. We are not thinking as an ecosystem. We're still focused on getting our business to understand where and what to monetize."

He then shared, "Design and iteration, in the context of cars, operate like physical design in manufacturing as opposed to the iterative approach of software. If we think about our cars as part hardware and part software, we can operate differently within that. We can then think about extending that idea to providing services that are more ancillary to that product." One could argue that, where the iPhone was a super cool device that became a powerful ecosystem, Tesla is still in the cool device phase and hasn't yet become an ecosystem, meaning there is still space for established automotive companies to lead in the ecosystem space.

Our conversation ended with another point that was critical to how the company would evolve continuously. He said, "How can we get enough data back from the cars to make better cars in the same way that Formula 1 continuously updates their cars? And how can we use that data for other areas of the business like marketing, so that we can move from a generic brand promise to a specific set of messages about the car?" These comments and insights stood out for me because they were a perfect example of what we'll explore next: the diverse set of capabilities required to create value through digital.

After years of work with clients across multiple industries, what follows are the five capability areas that, in concert, will enable you to evolve in sync with changing customer behavior and technology. What you will not find is an analysis of the most disruptive technologies and their impact on your business. We all know that the pace of technological change would quickly make that perspective outdated. This is about surfacing the fundamental capabilities that you will continue to build on and evolve to create powerful digital products, services, and experiences. These are your SPEED capabilities:

- Strategy: developing and testing your hypothesis on priority value pools
- Product: evolving at pace and scale
- Experience: how you can enable value for customers
- Engineering: delivering on your promise, at pace and at scale
- Data: validating your hypotheses and uncovering insights for constant iteration

What you'll start to see is that these capabilities are the ingredients that come together in the value creation life cycle, the PS How. While your Strategy capability may certainly be able to Ignite and Hunt for opportunity areas and potential markets, when combined with Product, Experience, Engineering, and Data, you can suddenly go from identifying a potential area of opportunity to rapidly prototyping, testing, and bringing it to market. In each set of activities of the life cycle you'll have various permutations that will allow you to operate like those digital organizations described earlier.

Over the next several chapters, we'll explore the role each of these plays in creating value. You'll also get a window into how they are evolving and what the potential is within each. Then, in the final section of the book, we'll talk about the many avenues for bringing these to life. No, you don't have to go it alone. In fact, your digitally native competitors don't do everything in-house for a reason, and neither should you. More on that later. Now, on to the SPEED capabilities.

### DBT Takeaway: The BHAGs of Digital Business Transformation

It's possible for any established business to get lost in their transformation – to stray from the original goal or to let the wrong approach hinder your forward progress. It's why the two BHAGs that I stress through this book serve as the parallel rails to keep you on track: one is continuous change and the other is value creation.

Your objectives and outcomes are destinations that you'll pass along the way, but it's the two BHAG rails that will keep you heading in the right direction as you make a host of other decisions necessary to maintain forward momentum.

The first BHAG, developing the muscle of continuous change, will be made easier by following the PS How frame laid out in this chapter. There are other decisions you will need to make along the way to ensure successful digital business transformation, including the way in which you build your transformation team: what size, what level of seniority and influence, is it sufficiently cross-functional, where can it be enhanced by bringing in a partner ecosystem?

The second, constructing the capability to identify and realize value, is where five key capability areas come into play. The following chapters in this book are designed to help you get those SPEED capabilities, Strategy, Product, Experience, Engineering, and Data, up to strength. Individually, and together, these play a key role in the value creation life cycle.

# CHAPTER 6

# Strategy

## Swarm Intelligence

For most first-time visitors to a foreign country, their first step on new soil can be sensory overload – the people, the colors, the sounds, the smells. Yet if they have landed in Delhi, Naples, or Istanbul, nothing seems to jolt the system like that first ride from the airport to the hotel. If there are traffic rules in these cities, it is very hard to tell. A cursory glance makes it appear that each motorist is operating in isolation. Yet, there is a method to the madness. Look a little closer and you'll see that drivers are following other individual drivers to get from point A to point B until they need to change course or they finally veer off.

In nature, you can witness a behavior known as swarm intelligence, where decentralized, self-organizing players operate as a collective. Think of bees and ants. Within a swarm of bees or a colony of ants, you have independent insects that act in concert with the whole. In the 1950s, a scientist named Pierre-Paul Grasse introduced a new concept within social insect societies called "stigmergy."[1] What he observed was that when one of the insects veered from the rest of the group, it left behind traces in the environment that actually changed the future actions of the rest of the group. More interestingly, these new actions were triggered through mutual awareness, not any direct coordination from one insect to the next. There was no centralized planning, control, or communication; they were just constantly learning from and adapting to one another.

Swarm intelligence and stigmergy are most commonly applied in a digital context to the fields of artificial intelligence (AI), machine learning, and robotics. I would argue, however, that we are in a moment where it is also having a direct impact on strategy as a whole. Let's explore what this looks like both proactively and reactively across the consumer and business landscapes today.

Were you to go back to the late 1990s when Amazon was just an online bookseller, part of its site design was to incorporate review pages where customers could comment on books and exchange ideas. By the late 1990s and early 2000s, those reviews became a key competitive advantage for Amazon. By the mid-2000s, *Business Insider* estimated that the "Was this helpful to you?" feature on the website accounted for over $2.7 billion in revenue alone. Today, it's hard to imagine purchasing just about anything without a review, whether it's on a retail site or one of the multitude of YouTube videos on anything from buying toothpaste to buying a car.[2]

Reactively, this one feature has influenced consumer expectations across a number of industries. In 2004, former PayPal employees Jeremy Stoppelman and Russel Simmons created Yelp after Stoppelman caught the flu and could not find any reviews for local doctors.

The experience triggered an idea to create an online review site where users would e-mail in their request for a recommendation and the answers would be posted on the site. The process was somewhat convoluted. The idea never fully took off, but through the process they discovered that people would include unsolicited reviews of their favorite local businesses. So, Stoppelman and Simmons decided to go in another direction. "I remember the moment that Russ said, 'There should be a way for you to write your own reviews without asking questions,'" Stoppelman recalled.[3] Through Yelp, Stoppelman and Simmons took the idea of reviews, applied it to small businesses, and built a social network on top of it.

Today, the review functionality is a critical component of the trustworthiness not just of Amazon and Yelp, but of most companies. Managing it (including managing the manipulation and legitimacy of the reviews themselves) has become critical. This is swarm intelligence and stigmergy playing out across digital companies.

## The Role of Strategy

Within established businesses, the function of strategy itself is undergoing a transformation. The primary orientation of strategy within most companies has always centered on value creation through competitive differentiation: the classic “where to play” and “how to win.” Until 10 to 20 years ago, the competitive set was well known, and for most established companies the barriers to entry in their industry were significant enough to create the economic moat extolled by Warren Buffett.

When the primary competitive threats began increasingly to come from new digital entrants, who were competing through completely different value propositions and business models, it created uncertainty and disruption around traditional competitive analysis. Your biggest competition is no longer defined by scale but by who is meeting the needs of your customers most effectively and by their ability to operationalize that into an effective business model. In turn, your primary strategic focus has to be on your customer, and your value is not just in the analysis, or even in developing a road map, but rather it is in your ability to test, learn, refine, and successfully bring to market.

Established companies face challenges that new digital entrants simply do not have to contend with. The biggest of these is how to transform a business while running that business. Strategy has arguably always played a critical role in setting the North Star for the direction of the company. In the context of transformation, this has never been more important given the balance between supporting the current model and moving to a new one.

As we explore the role of strategy, you will see that the high-level choices around aspiration, “where to play”, and “how to win” are still relevant. It is when you go a level deeper that we see there are specific considerations all companies should think about in relation to operating as a digital business.

## Anchor Strategy on Your Customer, Not Your Competition

The question “What is our winning aspiration?” has long been the starting point of strategic analysis. This ties to the purpose and vision of the organization and the questions that determine “Who do you want to be?” and “What value do you aim to create in the world?” The approach is as relevant today as it was when A. G. Laffley, former CEO of Proctor & Gamble, and Roger Martin, Strategist and Dean of Rotman Business School, introduced it in 2013’s *Playing to Win* as well as

| | |
|---|---|
| Visa | To be the best way to pay and be paid, for everyone, everywhere |
| Nestlé | Enhancing quality of life and contributing to a healthier future |
| Walmart | To save people money so they can live better |
| Bank of America | Help make financial lives better through the power of every connection |
| Proctor & Gamble | We will provide branded products and services of superior quality and value that improve the lives of the world's consumers, now and for generations to come |
| Novartis | Discover new ways to improve and extend people's lives |

**FIGURE 6.1** Evolution of business purpose statements

in the years preceding its publication, when the thinking was shaping applied strategy.

Have you noticed how large enterprises today ground their purpose in a customer orientation? If you look at the purpose statements of some of the best-known brands in Figure 6.1, you can see the shift happening.

Customer-oriented vision statements are the most powerful because they anchor to customer needs, which in turn can be used to shape your digital vision. The combination of connecting the purpose you serve in a customer's life to the solutions you are able to create through your digital capabilities becomes a space fertile with transformational opportunity.

In traditional business sequence, the next step would be to identify "where to play": the markets, product categories, or consumer groups that you will choose to focus on. This, however, is the point at which digital starts to turn things on their head.

## Determine "Where to Play" by Looking at Your Market Differently (the D-3 Model)

In early 2020, Publicis Sapient was speaking with the CEO of a global jewelry company. His business had started its journey to become more digital and was making progress on its digital customer experience (CX) through updates to the website and omnichannel platform, investing in data-driven marketing, and transforming the entire IT delivery model. While these were each significant efforts in the company's evolution, he wanted to engage the board of directors to explore opportunities and set the direction for their digital business transformation. He had three questions that he wanted us to help answer:

- What parameters or definitions should we place around "digital" and "digital transformation"?
- What role should digital play in our entire business/value chain?
- What is required to deliver on the defined ambition?

What is critically important to recognize is that these are not technology questions; they are questions about competitiveness.

In the context of digital business transformation, "where to play?" is not a question just of markets and customer segments, but is about making explicit choices that will determine the kind of value you aim to produce through your digital capability.

Established companies have been "doing digital transformation" for a long time. There are three well-defined patterns in what we refer to as the D-3 model: defend, differentiate, or disrupt, illustrated in Figure 6.2. The choice of which of these paths best fits a company's transformation perspective will have a direct correlation to its capabilities as well as to the value pools it is able to pursue.

Let's start with defend. This is essentially business as usual. Your primary focus is on serving your existing markets and audiences while leveraging best practices. Through my work, I often see companies invest in specific solutions that will allow them to keep pace with their traditional competitors: programs such as investing in ecommerce, digital marketing, or operational IT.

Differentiation can be a very rich opportunity space for many organizations. This path can take you from advancing your existing processes to a blurring of the line between your digital and physical operations. From a jewelry client that invested in upgrading its Salesforce Commerce application to be more agile, to a car manufacturer that creates data-driven platforms in order to optimize the customer journey, what manifests in the space of differentiation is broad and impactful.

Choosing to disrupt is where you start to lean into the full scope of digital business transformation. A hospitality client of ours had

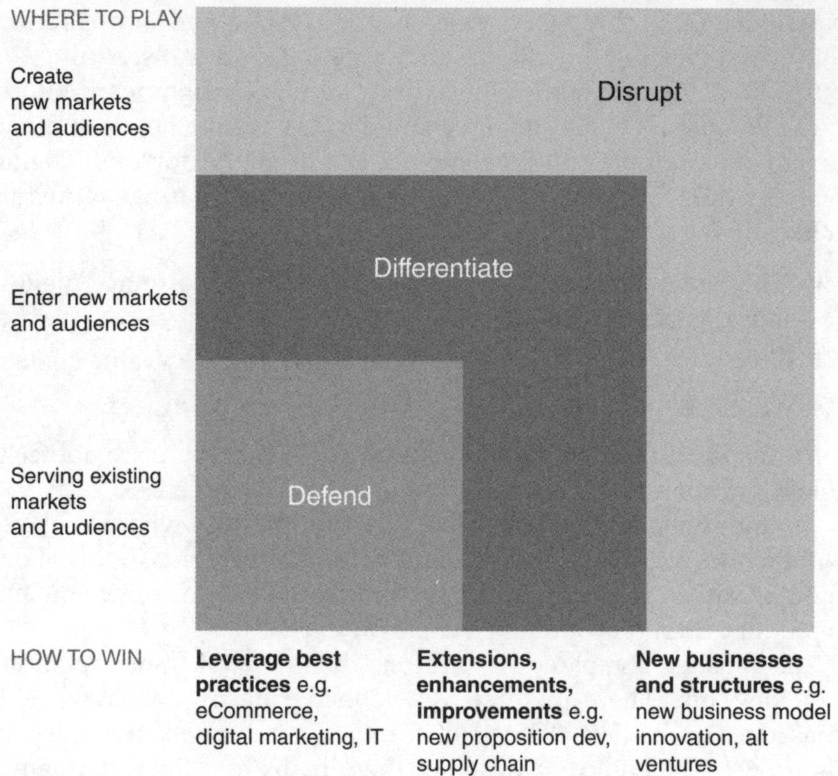


**FIGURE 6.2** The D-3 Model: Defend, Differentiate, Disrupt

identified new, adjacent markets where it could create value and was acquiring the capabilities that could supplement a new offer. The company had even created a vision of a connected platform that would differentiate its offering in the market. Although its initial efforts were not connected as strongly as they could have been, the business was still progressing under a shared vision.

What sets differentiation and disruption apart is that when you choose to disrupt you are creating new markets and audiences. Disruption also requires you to reach the decision that you are fundamentally going to change the way your company operates and produces value. This space can range from implementing agile across your capabilities all the way to zero-based design where you reimagine your business from the ground up just as a digitally native company would do.

# "How to Win": View Your Transformation as a Portfolio of Moves

An organization's strategy capability plays a critical role in setting its transformation objectives in the context of the economic model of the business. Whether you choose to defend, differentiate, disrupt, or some combination thereof, digitally transforming your business will require a portfolio of moves to get there. Each of these are choices that have implications for the business. What's important to remember here is that you don't have to pick just one. Your transformation can involve a combination. Figure 6.3 illustrates what this might look like when applied to customer journey transformation.

This provides a great illustration of the different value pools that can be addressed as part of a transformation program. These value pools can center on the customer, the business, or a mix and can include cost measures, capability investment, and innovative growth opportunities. The Hunt activities of the "PS How" value life cycle that we explored in the previous chapter is where your strategy team, in partnership with your other capability areas, starts to identify and prioritize value pools to determine which will drive the greatest outcomes. Now you have your North Star for your transformation programs.

Now let's dive a little deeper into what these portfolio choices might look like in the context of a bank. Publicis Sapient was working with a

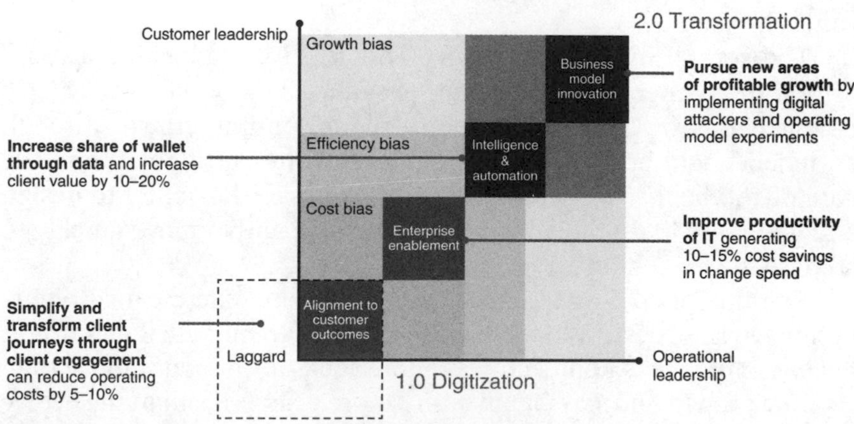


**FIGURE 6.3** Customer journey transformation

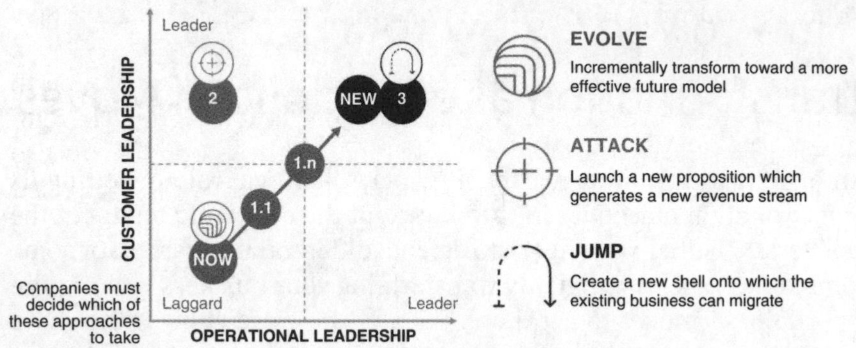


**FIGURE 6.4** Three models of transformation

large retail bank that was facing immediate competitive threats from fintech start-ups. At the same time, the bank was aware of the need to transform within its existing business, but faced the same challenges that many established businesses face around legacy technology, practices, and culture.

Three models of transformation emerged for how the bank could approach the challenge, which weighed the immediate threat with the longer-term transformation needs: evolve, attack, or jump. These models are illustrated in Figure 6.4.

The evolve approach focused on the long-term, taking a more gradual approach to both growth and cost-reduction transformation. Through evolve, the bank could address its capabilities, ways of working, and start to transform through a focus on customer-centric value streams.

The second option was attack. This involved launching a proposition to go after a new segment, provide a new service, or enter a new geography. Attack focused on driving top-line growth through an independent business that was intentionally partitioned from the core of the bank. This would give the necessary flexibility to design and operate it like a digitally native company, and to move quickly to address the fintech threat.

The final model was jump where the bank could create a highly optimized shell of the model that they wanted to migrate their current business into. This approach was more focused on bottom-line than top-line growth and was significantly more aggressive than the evolve model. It allowed the company to target a step-change in operations and customer experience and jump directly into new strategic platforms and ways of working. Along the way, the shell would give them the structure to reduce connections to the existing business.

What the portfolio approach allowed the bank to do was then to decide where it wanted to place its bets and how it wanted to allocate investment across some combination of these options. It also provided the flexibility to decide whether these allocations happened at a company level or within specific business units.

## Build "Your" Capabilities: The Partner Ecosystem

Strategy has always played a direct role in choices about how to build capabilities: from mergers and acquisitions, to decisions on how to build internally, to partnership choices. Never has this role been more critical than it is today.

Digital businesses are in a constant state of learning and adapting. Think back for a moment to those concepts of swarm intelligence and stigmergy. We are all familiar with Nest thermostats. Creating the first Nest product required bringing together learning technology that allowed Nest to program itself based on your habits: sensors from the medical industry so it could turn the temperature down when you weren't at home; lessons from the open-source software community; and electronics from the smartphone industry to make it low-cost, low-power, and high-performance. On top of this was exceptional product design to make Nest both visually appealing and easy to use.[4]

In the traditional model, most of the process from creation to realization would happen in-house. That is no longer the case today. As the rate of change has increased around us, it is impossible for one company to hold all the capabilities that it needs to innovate solutions. This is where partner ecosystems play an important role on creating adaptability, innovation, and scale.

First, customer needs are continuously evolving. Go back to those characteristics of digital businesses and the first is clarity on the need they are serving. Knowing what that need is starts with identifying those pain points that haven't been addressed. Co-creation has become an increasingly powerful application of the partnership ecosystem.

Digitally native companies have been operating in this way, many since inception. As have your partners. Publicis Sapient has an ecosystem of partners such as Adobe, Google, Microsoft, and Salesforce that we leverage to expand what we can bring to clients. These partnerships are not just about implementing technology; they are built around intellectual property that addresses specific customer solutions.

Partnership ecosystems are also multidirectional. They provide access and stickiness to customers as well as customer insights that go beyond any of their individual players. This gives you a more robust view into identifying what potential pain points could be served while also creating more visibility into how that is happening.

Whether you are using an ecosystem of partners to accelerate your digital business transformation, deliver new products and services, or create entirely new markets, partners will be key to advancing how you provide value for your customers and your business. Finally, in an environment that is rapidly evolving, partnership ecosystems provide access to talent and capabilities that may be difficult to acquire and scale. Many do even more than that.

As you move up the spectrum of defend, differentiate, and disrupt (D-3), the role of your partnerships will likely expand. If your focus is on defending, your partners may play a key role in value creation for your business by improving the systems and ways of working for your teams. If you are differentiating, partners can connect in new capabilities to round out differentiated offers for customers. At the disruption level, partners can become equals in the creation of platforms that provide mutual benefit to both parties.

Intellectual property and accelerator assets are another key consideration in the design of a partnership ecosystem. In October 2018, the analyst firm Gartner made a bold prediction. The company claimed that, by 2030, 80% of financial firms will either go out of business or be rendered irrelevant by new competition, customer behaviors, and advances in technology.[5] Today, banks face a new set of competitors including non-bank financial institutions and fintech companies that are disrupting the financial services landscape. The key reason for their success is their ability to anticipate customer needs and deliver the right products and services that traditional providers are too slow to create, also known as anticipatory banking.

Delivering on the anticipatory banking idea requires the ability to combine AI, machine learning, and behavioral science to help customers improve their financial well-being. How many established banks have the capability in-house to do that? This is where accelerators become a key part of the ecosystem that delivers at pace and scale. In a world where your ability to learn is as important, if not more important, than what you know, your partner ecosystems are a key ingredient for learning, adapting, and bringing your ideas to reality. Your strategy capability helps you to assess your partners, understanding both their capabilities and the accelerator assets they bring to bear to help guide what makes the most sense in terms of fit for delivering on the ideas you have planned.

## Bringing Products to Market: The Elusive Product-Market Fit

Much of what has been talked about in this chapter could be classified as sitting at the level of corporate strategy – covering the high-level choices that a company makes on what it wants to be, where it wants to play, and how to get there. Strategy certainly plays a core role at this level, but it also plays a central role in creating the grounding hypothesis on how to bring products and services to market.

Go back for a moment to the "PS How" life cycle. As value is created in your business, there is the Ignite phase which centers on getting stakeholder alignment on the need for transformation. You could argue that much of the D-3 analysis would sit here. You also have the Hunt phase, where you are searching for value-creating opportunities.

During the Hunt activities of the life cycle, you'll often find multiple capabilities coming together to map consumer need to potential products and markets. Imagine for a moment a scenario where data uncovers the potential opportunity for a consumer packaged goods (CPG) company to provide direct-to-consumer services for cleaning supplies. Strategy would come in and, working with the other SPEED capability areas, would determine the product-market fit. What is the product, where is there a market for it, and what's the business model to deliver it? Through pilots and testing, strategy would continue to be involved in the process to determine the viability of building, scaling, and taking the product to market.

Where strategy was once a capability that ran fairly independently of the rest of the business, today it is an inextricable piece of an integrated set of capabilities. It plays a pivotal role in creating the North Star to guide the choices for the business, while partnering with other capability areas to create products that meet the needs of today's consumers through compelling business models. What's exciting in this space is the expanding opportunity to leverage new and existing partners to advance what's possible for today's established companies, and to bring new solutions to market.

## DBT Takeaway: Strategy

Successful digital business transformation requires a different understanding of, and approach to, your strategy capability and the role it plays in your organization. It should guide your "where to play" and "how to win" but also how you determine funding, connect capabilities, and bring new products and services to the right market, profitably.

One of the first shifts your strategy capability must make is to move your organization's primary strategic focus away from your competition and toward your customer: Are you meeting their needs consistently, and are you operationalizing that strategic shift? Your digital vision should connect the purpose you serve in a customer's life to the solutions you can create from your digital capabilities.

Strategy should never sit isolated in a digital tower; in order to truly deliver on its potential in the transformation of your organization, strategy should be getting its hands dirty in a number of areas:

- Think about how you win. Is it best to evolve through incremental transformation, to attack a new and discrete business opportunity, jump in the direction of an entirely new business model, or to pursue a combined, concurrent approach to these options?
- Recognize that your business is not digitally native and you have an existing business to run. Consider how you might fund your transformation through a portfolio approach to defend, differentiate, and disrupt. Making a series of bets can help de-risk your overall portfolio while creating space for innovation.
- A partner ecosystem is key to unlocking value for your customers and your business. Today, it is near impossible to hold all the capabilities needed to innovate solutions within one company. Which partners can you bring in to plug your capability gaps and play a part in co-creation?

# CHAPTER 7

# Product

## Operating in Constant Beta

For most of our clients there is a strategy function; for a few there is an experience function; but for all there is some version of a product function. Visit the website of any major corporation and you will get a sense for whether their P&L is structured by products, regions, or some combination.

For many established businesses, product-based P&Ls are where transformation efforts begin. They are often the most natural place to inject change because they are the most direct connection point between customer, go to market, and capability. The challenge is that most of these product structures were designed for a different time.

Neil McElroy is most known for his roles as president of Procter & Gamble (P&G) and as US secretary of defense under President Dwight D. Eisenhower. On May 13, 1931, he was a junior executive at P&G managing the advertising and promotion of Camay soap. At the time, advertising, and sales were managed as distinct functions, and he found himself competing with Ivory Soap, one of P&G's own brands, for money and attention. He was making a pitch for a couple of new hires for his team and wrote an 800-word memo arguing for a brand-based structure that would allow each brand to have the proper team, budget, and focus to compete successfully. McElroy argued that there needed to be teams focused on single brands under a single owner, what he called "Brand Men" at the time, who had full accountability for a brand from advertising to sales and promotion and overall performance. The brands would become distinct businesses able to more effectively differentiate themselves. He got his hires, but more importantly, his memo initiated P&G's restructure into a brand-centric organization and influenced how most corporations would manage their brands to this day.[1]

In the late 1930s, McElroy became an advisor at Stanford University, where he influenced two up-and-coming entrepreneurs named Bill Hewlett and David Packard. Bill and Dave would build off of McElroy's approach to brand management and start to more clearly shift to product management, structuring Hewlett-Packard (HP) around key product groups, but creating a stronger connection to customer value and incorporating product development and manufacturing as part of the responsibilities of the product manager. In *The HP Way* internal booklet from 1980, they describe their customer objective: "To provide products and services of the greatest possible value to our customers, thereby gaining their respect and loyalty."[2]

As Bill and Dave were building Hewlett-Packard in the United States, Taiichi Ohno and Eiji Toyoda were taking the just-in-time manufacturing approaches of post-war Japan to create the Toyota Production System and the Toyota Way. They introduced two key ideas that influence product management to this day: *Kaizen*, continuous improvement; and *Genchi Genbutsu*, "going to the source," or checking facts yourself to make sure you have the right information you need to make a good decision.[3] The team at HP adopted these principles into their work, creating an approach to product that combined the brand orientation from P&G, the focus on customer value and development they were building within HP, and the ideas of lean manufacturing and continuous improvement from Toyota. From 1943–1993, the tenets of the HP Way sustained 50 years of 20%+ year-over-year growth, and the ideas and approaches within it laid the foundation for many of the cultures and approaches you see in Silicon Valley today.

While these stories are decades old, you can still see the influence of each of these approaches in businesses today. The challenge for many of our clients who are still operating in brand-based organizations is how to transform while managing organizational silos. Meanwhile, they are competing with technology companies, where the ideas of brand, consumer, and continuous innovation are baked into the accountability of the product manager. This is not only a different orientation to the role, but the system around the role is designed to operate at a different speed addressing different outcomes.

## The Relentless Hunt for Value

The holy grail of product management is creating the capability to repeatedly produce products and services that achieve product-market fit, where you create products that customers want to buy, have identified the audience that wants to buy them, and have designed a business model that compels that audience to buy your product. Many products (and companies) have fallen by the wayside because they only had one or two pieces of this. Success relies on all three. In the strategy chapter, we talked about the role strategy plays in collaborating with the other SPEED capabilities to shape product-market fit. This is precisely why product is a team sport and also why this book is grounded on the interrelationship between the five SPEED capability areas.

What is easy to understand is the need for collaboration. What is much more challenging within established businesses is to create the system where both the collaboration and work of these five capability areas are happening concurrently.

The simplest way to think about this is, at any given moment, your business has to be simultaneously identifying and realizing value. Identifying value is more than just surfacing ideas; it requires tight cross-functional coordination across the five capability areas to identify, shape, prototype, and test the viability of the idea. Realizing value is how you scale these ideas through delivery and then bring them to market or to your internal organization. This is where the PS How provides a framework to navigate how value is created, which you can then use to piece together the capabilities needed along the way.

## The Inconvenient Truths of Product

Today, the combination of Moore's Law accelerating the rate of technological change and the unpredictable nature of how people are adapting to those changes has completely disrupted product development. Our clients are constantly looking for answers to questions like how do you get ideas into market as quickly as possible? How do you pivot when you realize your guess around how customers would react is not exactly correct? The project-driven approaches of old are not as effective in this new world.

In his book *Inspired: How to Create Tech Products Customers Love*, Marty Cagan shares what he calls the "two inconvenient truths of product":[4]

1. At least half of our ideas are just not going to work.
2. It will take several iterations to get the implementation of these ideas to the point where they deliver the necessary business value.

Today, 70% of digital transformations fail and companies are left with little to show for considerable investments.[5] There are a couple of dynamics that consistently show up in failed transformations. First is the "watermelon effect," where the service-level agreements (SLAs) all look green on the outside, but inside the program is red and the efforts are not producing the desired business results. The challenge is that as much as companies proclaim they use Agile and Lean methods, they consistently revert back to waterfall processes with handoffs from one area to the next. This approach then creates a negative, reinforcing loop focused more on the output of the projects versus the outcomes for the business. It also creates what's referred to as "technical debt," where companies take what appears to be the easier, shorter path instead of the path that will produce the right outcomes, resulting in additional cost to rework the solution.

As he reflected on the most successful product teams he'd seen, Cagan shared three principles they all had in common:[6]

1. **Risks are tackled up front, rather than at the end.** This addressed what is one of the core problems with the waterfall approach: the product is only tested and validated at the end of the development process, creating much greater overall risk. Cagan argues that the strongest teams assess risk much earlier in the development process so they can address it in the final product.
2. **Products are defined and designed collaboratively, rather than sequentially.** This is one of our core beliefs at Publicis Sapient as well. You cannot operate with the agility needed for today without collaboration built into your model. We believe that requires a deep connection across strategy, product, experience, engineering, and data. The partnership across is what creates the magic that produces products that are not only financially viable, but create customer and business outcomes.

3. **It's all about solving problems, not implementing features.** This comes back to that idea of outputs versus outcomes. Focusing on outcomes creates checks and balances to prevent the watermelon effect of project-oriented approaches.

## The Forces of Change in Product

This brings us back to those models of brand and product. The brand-based structure operates around long-range plans, typically measured in years. The product-based structure is designed to iterate, test, learn, and operate in continuous development. Making the switch between the two is one of the most challenging transformations our clients face. It's not just product development that's changing, but internal processes, like budgeting, that reinforce waterfall approaches also have to work in this way. This is where creating a model built for continuous improvement of the full product, both digital and physical, becomes critical.

Think about the way we used to manage projects. Every project manager would manage three variables: time, scope, and cost. How long will something take to do? What is it that we're doing? Tell me exactly what the requirements are, which is the scope. How much is this going to cost? Project managers have had this trifecta drilled into them from the time they started their careers. But in this world in which change is continuous, that management system is not working well. The reason is quite simple. When you think about trying to nail down what it is that you have to build and scope, essentially you do a lot of analysis up front. You do a lot of analysis that you might never use. By the time you actually get to building all of the things you thought you needed to build, the world has changed around you or customer expectations have changed.

When you think about time, any good project manager worth her salt is going to add buffer, which actually makes you slow because the project expands in size to fill all that available buffer. And the same is true of cost, where we tend to add buffer to the budgets and all of that buffer is consumed. This is illustrated in Figure 7.1.

So, what if instead of focusing on time, scope, and cost, we focus on **speed**: How fast can we go from an idea all the way to putting it into the world? How can we do that with **quality** so that whenever we do it, we are not breaking things? In addition, how do we make sure

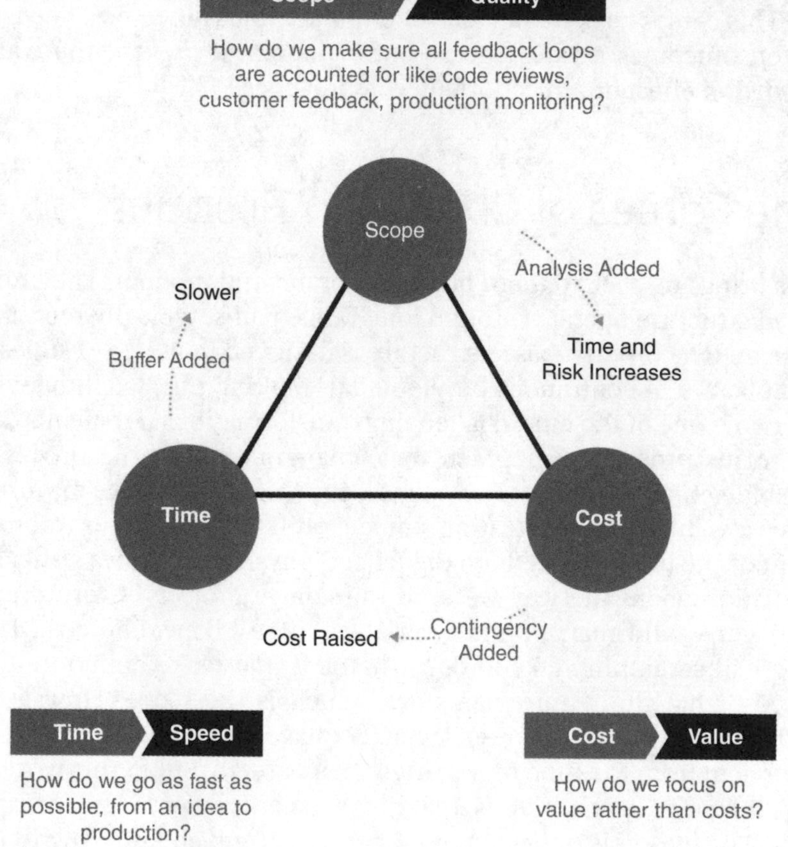


**FIGURE 7.1** Model for enacting change quickly and at scale

we're not just completing the scope but delivering the **value** to the customers and to the business?

When you make this shift to speed, quality, and value, you gain the ability to move at the speed of disruptive change in the face of uncertainty.[7]

## Agile, Lean, and DevOps

Whether we're talking about product, experience, engineering, or any particular aspect of transformation, there are some terms that get commonly batted around the principles of Agile, Lean, and DevOps, as seen in Figure 7.2, will underpin many of your organization's

● **Organizational Design**

With a fast pace of change, it is important that the organization adjusts to support through engineering governance, adopting a value-driven approach and becoming product aligned.

● **Technology & Engineering**

Core to the work where teams apply interventions that span across DevOps, infrastructure, application architecture, and quality engineering.

● **Communication, Culture, & Capability**

Ensures the waves of change are sustainable by the organization. These activities are also essential to create a pull for organic growth.

● **Product & Process**

Play a role in ensuring that a data-driven culture is adopted, measuring not only internal but external outcome-focused metrics. It allows organizations to adopt agile ways of working. Product management keeps customer needs at the heart of everything.

**FIGURE 7.2** The principles of Agile, Lean, and DevOps

capabilities. It's important we clarify what these are here, because each of these concepts is key to how product management is executed.

The first is Agile. We've spoken a lot about the rate of change and uncertainty. Agile is a set of frameworks, practices, and principles designed to give teams the agility to respond to change. Agile is based on Lean, key values:

- Individuals and interactions over processes and tools
- Working software over comprehensive documentation
- Customer collaboration over contract negotiation
- Responding to change over following a plan

The critical characteristic of Agile is the focus on the cross-functional team and how to work in a way that is inclusive of change and uncertainty within your development process.

Where Agile enables adaptability to change through cross-functional teams, Lean methodologies are primarily focused on reducing waste so those teams can be more effective in driving outcomes. In the context of product management, this is a really important concept. Think back to the inconvenient truths of product: half of your ideas won't work and you will need multiple iterations to get something ready to take to market. You could easily fall prey to the trappings of technical debt or, on the opposite end of the spectrum, blow your speed and agility. Ultimately, you could lose your window to capture the opportunity with your customer or market. Truly applying Lean in a digital context requires getting to the place where your capabilities are working concurrently and collaboratively to create high-value products.

It's quite easy to imagine a start-up building itself from the ground up anchoring on Agile and Lean methodologies. But for established businesses with deep-seated operational silos, those propositions are much more challenging. What DevOps provides is a way for companies to produce software faster and with higher quality by directly addressing the organizational silos and blockers. It's an approach that creates stronger collaboration between software development and IT operations teams, provides stronger connections to your lines of business and customers, and improves your organization's ability to produce continuous software delivery.

Within each of these three approaches you will find a number of methodologies and approaches for how to execute. The key is to find the ones that work in the context of your business and ultimately drive your ability to deliver value consistently, with quality, and repeatedly for your customers.

## Banking Case Study: Transforming Product

In 2014, Publicis Sapient was in discussions with one of the United Kingdom's leading retail and commercial banks, about its digital transformation. The digital CIO at the time and transformation director described the effort as "taking digital and making it a change agent for the group rather than solely for the channel."

The company had just come off a three-year customer experience transformation program and was starting to see the broad implications of digital on the business. Though the customer experience work was a start, it could never fully position them for a rapidly changing digital world. Leadership had a number of "aha" moments through their journey.

First was one of the most important shifts in any digital business transformation: the shift to customer. The CIO and head of digital and transformation shared, "We were solving the classical online problem rather than focusing on customer experience across touchpoints, policies, and procedures. We needed to stop thinking about digital channels and approach customer problems holistically." Yes! By making the shift to a customer focus, they started to see where there was friction in the experience not just in the front end but across the value chain. They also were seeing the limitations of their current capabilities.

Second, customer experience became a core tenet of the strategy. They realized the impact it had on driving growth and retention and made a deliberate choice to focus on it, especially in its business banking, financial planning and retirement, and unsecured customer lending businesses. By creating a more friction-free experience they could improve performance.

Finally, though Agile methods had been introduced in the organization, it was far from Agile at scale. The clients knew they had to fundamentally change their ways of working and wanted a partner to help guide how they built this capability and ways of working in the business.

Taking on a transformation of this scale is incredibly daunting. One of the hardest choices is how to begin. In this client's case, we focused on the transformation of 10 customer journeys end-to-end based on cost to the group and importance to customers. These 10 journeys included some of the most core products and services within the bank. This by nature ensured a foundational product orientation to the work.

The product-based journeys were a natural entry point into changing ways of working because they had a clear tie to both the customer and operating model within the company. We created what we called the "enterprise startup," a concept that signaled a new way of working within those product groups. The "enterprise startup" would operate differently from the norm at the time, specifically focusing on driving speed within the organization while breaking organizational silos. It was guided by the ideas of applying design thinking, emphasizing speed over perfection, focusing on end-to-end service design, advocating for internal and external transformation, and building an innovation ecosystem.

One thing about the transformation that was critical was the client team's recognition that this was not just about technology. They knew that what they were transforming was their culture, organization, technology, and metrics. This brings us back to the idea of shifting from scope, time, and cost to quality, speed, and value. This is exactly what they used to guide the transformation program:

- *From Scope to Quality*. They replaced traditional approaches to scoping the product work up front. Instead, design and delivery teams focused on software quality, incorporating user feedback on usability and functionality into the development and delivery process.
- *From Time to Speed*. Instead of focusing on large projects, they created an architecture of loosely coupled microservices and private cloud environments integrated with the group's back-end systems, giving them multiple entry points to rapidly evolve the customer experience.
- *From Cost to Value*. They completely shifted their orientation toward budgeting, designing it for an environment of continuous iteration where journey improvements are reviewed on a weekly basis. Product owners pitch for additional budget on a monthly basis, with the funding structure designed to mimic venture capital firms.

Over a three-year transformation program, the client was able to start to make the shift so the new operating model established through these 10 journeys became part of their business as usual. The bank started producing new and improved digital propositions, with Forrester recognizing it for having the most capable retail mobile banking services in the United Kingdom. The shift to customer value began producing results not just with customers but internally as well where it was able to reduce the time it takes corporate customers to update employee files from 21 days to 24 hours, resulting in a 78% increase in positive customer feedback and 40% increase in the capacity of employees to focus on value-add activities. On the business side, the bank was also able to increase the path to purchase for credit applications by 40% and raise average loan amounts by £700. But, perhaps the most powerful outcome was around speed. It went from a 12–18-month development cycle to get a product live down to 4–5 months.

Your product capability plays a critical role in bringing all capability areas together in service of the customer, addressing known needs and unknown needs, and doing it all continuously over time. And, let's face it, the investment you make in product is one of the hardest, yet most pivotal choices any executive will make because it is more than just investing in a capability; it is fundamentally reshaping your business model, who you are as a company, and the level of value you provide to your customers. At a time when industry and business model disruption is the norm, established companies have to start bravely taking these steps forward. In the words of the late Harvard Business School Professor Clayton Christensen, "Breaking an old business model is always going to require leaders to follow their instinct. There will always be persuasive reason not to take a risk. But if you only do what worked in the past, you will wake up one day and find that you've been passed by."[8]

## DBT Takeaway: Product

When you are able to make the organizational shift from a project mindset to a product mindset, you will have achieved one of the key leaps necessary to successful digital business transformation. The project-driven approaches of old are not effective in a digital world. The need now is to build a product capability that serves as connective tissue, bringing all capabilities together in service of the customer.

The holy grail here is to cultivate the capability to repeatedly develop products and services that achieve product-market fit. This is value identified, and then realized: your organization is able to create products that customers want to buy, has identified the audience that wants to buy them, and has designed a business model that compels that audience to buy your product.

In the product capability area, there are a few traps that established businesses regularly get snarled up in. Look out for and avoid these:

- Instead of focusing on time, scope, and cost, focus on speed, quality, and value. This gives you the ability to move at the speed of disruptive change in the face of uncertainty, and will deliver value both to customers and the business.
- Consider why a digital transformation might fail. Unmask old-school waterfall processes that just pay lip service to Agile, Lean methods. If the focus is more on outputs and handoffs than on shared outcomes for the business then you must course-correct!
- Beware "technical debt," where what appears to be the easier, shorter path is instead leading to the wrong, or zero, business outcome.

# CHAPTER 8

# Experience

## Everything in Your Business Contributes to Your Customer Experience

A few years ago, as part of my role chairing the annual conference of the Marketing Society, I organized a panel discussion between Jeremy Darroch, CEO of Sky Telecom, and Sir David Brailsford, general manager of the Team Sky cycling team. The topic of the conversation was driving behavioral change and productivity gains in cycling and in business.

In 2003, Brailsford was hired as the performance director by British Cycling, the organization that governed professional cycling for United Kingdom. At the time, the state of British cycling was pretty abysmal. In a period of more than 100 years, the British cycling team had only won one gold medal in the Olympics and had never won the Tour de France. Their reputation had become so bad that one of Europe's top bicycle manufacturers refused to sell them their bikes because they thought it would be bad for sales.

When Brailsford came in, he introduced a completely different approach to the team. He called it "the aggregation of marginal gains" and described it as follows: "The whole principle came from the idea that if you broke down everything you could think of that goes into riding a bike, and then improve it by 1%, you will get a significant increase when you put them all together."[1]

Instead of focusing purely on training the cyclists, he and his team engineered everything that was part of the cycling process to improve by that 1%: from redesigning bike seats to make them more comfortable and greasing the wheels to make them smoother, to changing the mattresses and pillows the team slept on to ensure better rest, hiring surgeons to teach them how to wash their hands to prevent illness, and testing massage gels to help speed up muscle recovery.

The results of the marginal gains approach: five years after Brailsford took on his role, the British Cycling team won 60% of the gold medals at the 2008 Olympic Games. Four years later they won nine golds at the London Olympics. Then, that same year, they went on to win their first Tour de France and would do the same in 2015, 2016, and 2017. Their run under Brailsford was the most successful in British Cycling's history.

Like marginal gains, your experience capability plays a central role in optimizing every component of what makes up your user experience, whether transformative in nature or marginal. Today, the capability is also changing as the medium of digital continues to expand.

## What Is Experience, Anyway?

One of the common misconceptions about experience is that it is synonymous with the "brand experience." Brand experience was seen as an extension of the branding and communications that a company put out, from outdoor to television. Over the years, this had evolved to include the physical experience of signage, layout of stores, and the design of packaging.

With the advent of the Internet, there was a clear shift to the idea of an interactive experience: something you could interact with primarily digitally, usually in the context of an early website. As websites evolved they were primarily a channel that was used to provide information about products, buy them, or transact with an organization, essentially connecting customers and the organization, but still as another channel.

With the iPhone and digitization of physical spaces, we saw physical spaces and digital experiences start to overlap. For anyone who works in retail, you may remember a decade ago when one of the biggest threats was "showrooming", consumers checking out a product in a brick-and-mortar store but then buying from an online retailer (ahem, Amazon). Though these worlds of physical and digital were overlapping, companies were still largely addressing them distinctly.

What was convenient about this marketing-oriented definition is that it was easy to understand and relatively easy to execute. You could focus your experience efforts on marketing and occasionally a specific sales channel or two, each managed distinctly, while the creation of products, services, and customer support continued to be managed through the processes the business always followed. In the early 2010s, companies still largely operated from the orientation of "How can we use experience to drive better awareness and conversion of our products through digital channels?"

Fast-forward to today and some fundamental shifts have happened in how we understand experience. The first is the orientation to customer. At this point, you are probably seeing a theme here. Remember those first two characteristics of digital companies: understanding the need they are serving and the value to the customer? This orientation has very different implications than anchoring to the product or service you provide. Now you may be saying, "Hold on, my company wouldn't be here if we didn't have a focus on the customer. The needs of the customer are what shape our products to begin with." And you would be absolutely right. The difference is now it's not just about how the products you sell better meet a need but how your company can identify and meet the needs of your customers more effectively.

This is directly connected to the second shift: Experience encompasses the entire customer journey and crosses organizational silos. Customers are increasingly expecting the interactions with brands to be frictionless. Amazing products have to be coupled with strong experiences which can only be created by connecting everything from what it is like walking into a physical location to the "unboxing experience" (i.e. the physical experience of beginning to use a product). More broadly, everything "above the glass" that customers see and interact with has to be connected to what's "below the glass," the internal functions that feed into those experiences. Whether you're selling financial products or groceries, creating compelling experiences that meet the needs of customers will stretch well into your organization. This end-to-end experience design is where digital natives compete incredibly effectively.

The third shift is centered on where digital enters the value creation process. Today, digital is part of the design toolkit when products, services, and experiences are conceived and evolved. This is very different from the days when it was a channel that was addressed after a product was already created. What's exciting is that the possibilities of what you can do now through digital have improved substantially from those early days a decade-plus ago. This is where that exponential rate of change works in our favor. Take, for instance, the multiple implications from data: Digital companies are designing every aspect of their customer journey with data capture in mind. This feeds their systems of value identification and realization, which nurtures their ability to change with the changing needs of their customers. That's pretty powerful.

Data and computation are also fundamentally evolving the experience capability itself. Moore's Law combined with the increase in storage capacity created the ability to apply AI and machine learning in ways that were still theoretical a decade ago. We'll explore this more in this chapter, but what it essentially does is create the ability for experience designers to move at a faster pace while leveraging computation in their designs themselves.

Finally, how we define what makes a great experience has also changed. It's no longer about the worlds we create around a product, but is much more closely anchored to how digital is applied to increase the usability and effectiveness for the customer. There are four characteristics we've identified that shape this – Light, Ethical, Accessible, and Dataful (LEAD) – that we'll explore in more detail.

To see how these four shifts play out today, let's step away for a moment from the natural inclination to explore a consumer-oriented company and look instead to a business-to-business (B2B) client in the highly specialized area of energy research and consultancy. It was an extraordinary company in many ways, which played a critical role in informing some of the key decisions companies made globally in the energy and natural resources sector. For example, decisions impacting things like the global energy supplies and the flow of oil and gas across the world. Or, say, the total value of oil and gas revenue from the territories that ISIS seized in northern Iraq and Syria in a few key months in 2014.

The tragedy was that all this advanced knowledge was being extracted and published just once a quarter, burned onto CDs, and then sent to IT representatives at the clients' organizations to be installed manually. Essentially, the company had the best data and the worst interface.

Beyond the interface though, its goal as a company was to supply the highest quality data to inform real decisions in the energy market. Now, let's pause for a moment and think about the need for decision making at pace. Clearly CDs were not an optimal choice. Nor were they addressing any of the four shifts we mentioned above.

Redesigning the user interface was not just about making the one billion rows of structured data and over 30,000 pages of unstructured data accessible online. It was also about designing it in a way where it could meet the needs of the end users making those day-to-day decisions (think real-time data), across silos, while also giving our client the visibility into how its customers were actually using the data itself. The data tool would play a key role in supporting the delivery of the client strategy in areas such as brand and client relationships; identification of the best growth opportunities; delivery of high-quality, differentiated, and integrated research products; and strong employee engagement. This is where bringing experience and digital into the value creation process became critical. Now the product experience was reflecting the brand purpose and intention.

Returning to the D-3 model, some might argue this was nothing more than "defend", the digitization of an existing product or service. I'd argue it is at the very least a "differentiation", embracing a new approach to understanding customer needs and value, using the latest technologies to deliver it. Its effect was "disruptive" by making the knowledge service relevant and available to a wider number of clients and driving up the user base by 500% and, as a byproduct, creating one of the biggest-ever data overlays on Google Maps.

The wide reach of experience is its greatest strength. It bridges the gap between your strategy and the capabilities that come together to form who you will become as a digital business and how you create value for your customers. And, as Brailsford did with the British Cycling team, it's about more than what any spectator would see in a race; it is all of the visible and invisible choices that contribute to the ultimate outcome. Every aspect of your company, whether customer facing or internal, shapes the customer experience and, as with the British Cycling team, every touch point working in concert can contribute to wholly different outcomes and the realization of your aspiration as a company.

## Orienting to the Customer

If there were a central anchor for experience it would be the customer. There is no company that more deftly brought a strategy to life through customer-led experience than Apple with the creation of the iPhone. Greg Christie, who headed Apple's Human Interface group, once said "Apple is best when it's fixing the things that people hate."[2]

With the iPhone, fixing the mobile phone experience was a two-year endeavor that required the hardware and software to work together, from having a single button with just a touchscreen to enabling Wi-Fi to the inertial scrolling functionality. Even the bounce that happens when you hit the end of a page – that happened because of an insight from one of the members of the user interface team, Bas Ording. "I thought my program wasn't running because I tried to scroll and nothing would happen. So that's when I started to think, 'How can I make it so you can see or feel that you're at the end?'" What's interesting about the development of the iPhone was the number of quick turnaround demos that happened on the path to market. The famous icons we are all accustomed to? Hashed out in a few hours.

In 2012, as the Olympic Games were taking place in London, I was honored to be invited to speak at a government-sponsored event that centered on the Olympics and United Kingdom's value in the world. Among the other speakers was British-born Jony Ive, then head of industrial design at Apple.

I had been an iPhone user since its launch five years earlier. In conversation, I commented that at this Olympic Games, the iPhone would fundamentally change the way in which people actually experienced the event and shared their experience. Instead of looking pleased with himself, a look of consternation crossed his face. "It's great to see that the iPhone is popular and important in people's lives," he said, "but the more I see that, the more I worry about whether it's as good as it can be, and how we can and have to improve on it."

In a single thought, Ive demonstrated not only that he had the drive for perfection that any great designer might have, but that he understood that even this most revolutionary of devices would have to constantly evolve, incorporating technological progress and customer expectations.

The preceding year, Apple co-founder Steve Jobs had died, and a few questions were being asked about the future of the company. This conversation with Jony Ive reassured me, at least, that through the Apple team's orientation to constantly evolving their products and services, they'd be just fine.

This process of connecting the idea, design, engineering, and experience to a powerful business proposition was the basis for one of the most revolutionary products in history. But what about the competitive response? This is where the digital moat becomes important. For most companies, going from where they are today to developing a product like the iPhone is a stretch to say the least. But what happens when an iPhone-like product or service enters your market? This is when your connected capability becomes critical. When Steve Jobs created the iPhone, he said he had a five-year lead relative to other phone manufacturers. In reality, it took six or seven years for competitors like HTC to make the HTC One. But once those competitors caught up, they found their own points of differentiation through screen size, cameras, and pricing. And today, while Apple is still wildly successful and dominant, it too has to prepare itself for changing competition and prepare for what's next, whether that's the Apple Watch, AirPods, or Apple TV.[3]

## Brand Is the Experience and Experience Is the Brand

In the late 1990s and early 2000s, much of the focus of our experience work was centered on the web. For clients at that time, the web was the centerpiece for creating a ubiquitous brand experience. As we were designing websites, we took disciplines like content strategy and information architecture to create the "above the glass" experience. Information architecture (IA) is the science of organizing and structuring the content of websites, web and mobile applications, and social media software. Without it, the web (and, in turn, client touch points) would contain an unwieldy amount of unstructured information. The interesting thing about IA is designing the systems of information required understanding the interdependencies among users, content, and context, which would often lead the sponsoring executive to ask, "Why is our org chart structured the way it is?"

Fast-forward a couple of decades and what sits in the organization "below the glass" is as much a part of the product and service design as what sits above. Experience is defined by anything and everything that touches a user of a system, a process, or a consumer and how much we can improve that person's satisfaction, ability to complete their task, and delight them wherever possible. When done well, it is multidisciplinary, with teams encompassing not just "experience" capability, but strategy, engineering, data, and product as well.

With product and service design the goal is to surface, design, and build ideas that will unlock value. If you look at the following diagram, it provides a simple lens through which you can start to identify areas of opportunity. It takes a customer-centric view, while thinking about the customer all the way through to the organization. Today you will find different companies that specialize in each quadrant, but when you think about the digital transformation of your business, you need to be able to do it all.

Once you've identified the opportunities for value or the change candidates (i.e. your ideas), as illustrated in Figure 8.1, you would go through a process to understand them in enough detail to implement, create requirements, and have a backlog of change. From that backlog you'd go through to implementation to take the product live.

Figure 8.2 shows how service design is used at the front stage of that life cycle, to find the opportunities and understand the value

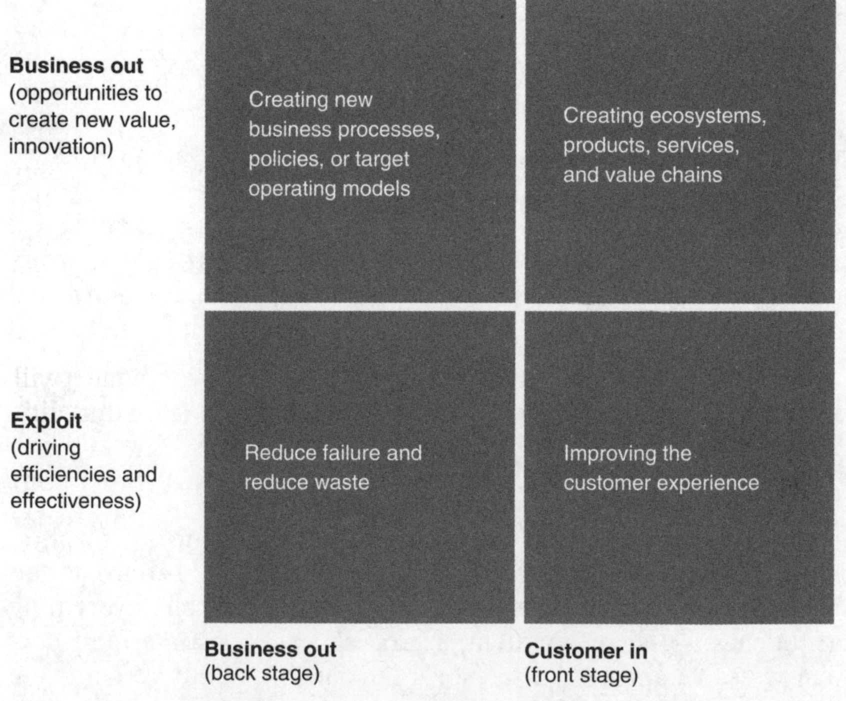


**FIGURE 8.1** Opportunities to create value

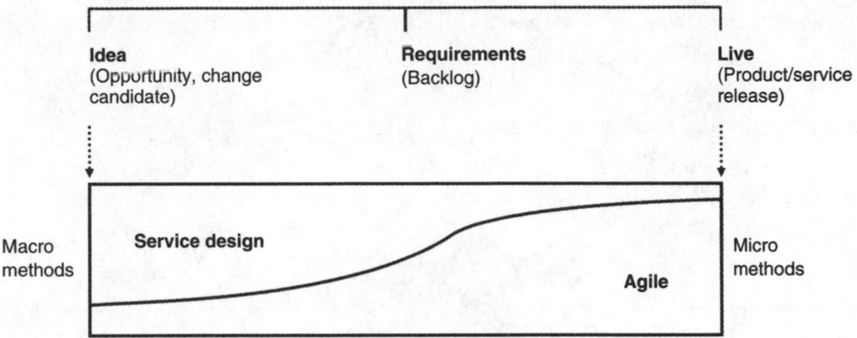


**FIGURE 8.2** Connecting service design to delivery

they represent and then how Agile methodologies are used along that journey to test and bring the ideas to market. Through Agile you create the regular rhythm to implement the ideas and take them live and incorporate micro methods like Lean and Six Sigma to bring them to life.

As you look at service design overall, there are four key components: design thinking, front stage/back stage, change candidates, and modeling for behavior as seen in Figure 8.3. Design thinking gives us the who and the why, allowing us to connect need to the company's purpose. Front stage/back stage allows you to look across the entire landscape of opportunities where you can create value: This is your broadest opportunity landscape. Those two areas then filter into the more specific change candidates where we can create value, including identifying our mixed backlog. The mixed backlog could include opportunities from any part of the business: policy change, process change, user experience, customer experience, technology, etc. Finally, you apply modeling to determine which of the change candidates will create the most value. This allows you to then test and learn and ultimately scale out into live environments.

These basic components serve as the foundation we will build from as we explore how Moore's Law combined with advances in computation, data, and AI, as well as rapid prototyping, are accelerating what the experience capability can do.

Let's look at an example. A cruise operator in 2009 wanted to use the Internet to get its business to leverage the web. The financial crisis had introduced huge cost pressures on its ability to market and sell cruises though physical locations. The company saw the web as a great

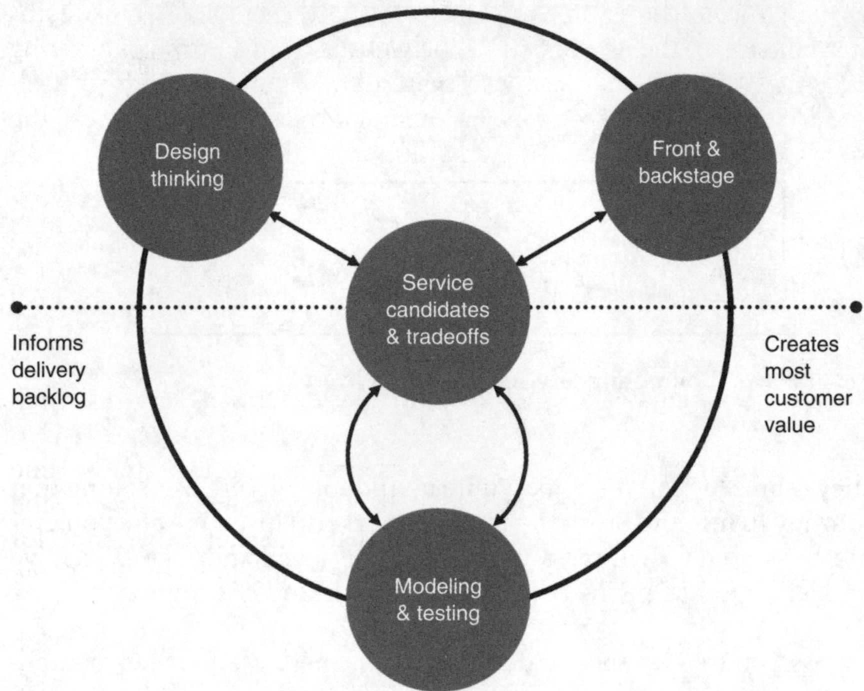


**FIGURE 8.3** Service design foundations

opportunity to shift these activities and reduce cost. It viewed digital as an "above the glass" marketing and sales channel.

We began the process to understand its audiences – for these cruises, this was a largely older demographic – and used techniques like ethnography and observation to see what they used the physical locations for. With these insights, we created an experience map effectively mapping out the entire journey of how people bought cruises. As we did, we also created a frame to understand the broader context of how the planned holiday trips mapped to their expectations of points in the process where they wanted or needed support.

It soon became pretty obvious that because a cruise was a big expensive purchase for most people, they were unlikely to buy online. However strong the website, it lacked the human reassurance they were seeking.

As we correlated our research to data in our client's business, one interesting fact about the economics of the process started to emerge: Its customers budgeted a fixed amount of money to spend per day on items from extras on the ship to onshore excursions. Our teams started to pivot the experience of the website from a purely marketing and sales channel that served research and buying the cruise itself to serving other parts of the customer journey as well, namely the purchase of add-on services like a dinner at the captain's table or an onshore excursion. These were all items that were relatively inexpensive in comparison to the cost of the cruise, which people felt much more comfortable buying online.

The redesigned site was successful. Customers could research a cruise before going into a physical location to book it, and come back to the website and access tools like calendars and schedulers to help them manage their time on-board and buy add-on services. Then something remarkable happened: Despite now buying these add-ons, their spending on the cruise stayed the same! Because they came from different budgets over the course of the year, by focusing on the broader experience, we were able to create a better experience for the customer, which in turn created more value for our client, the cruise operator.

Fast-forward to today, and the experience encompasses so much more. Customer insights have created more options from the booking process to the on-board experience. Customers can select cabins based on their specific views. Boarding passes are accessed via your mobile device, which can now be used in a multitude of ways onboard: including unlocking your room, providing access to particular areas of the ship based on what you have paid for, and controlling your entertainment preferences. And, now, the instrumentation of the ship itself can monitor footfall traffic in real time in various parts of the ship and tailor and market specific services to people in those areas.

Executing this experience required creating a platform with an event-driven architecture that created a unified experience for customers, leveraging multiple functions within the organization. Every part of the customer journey was accessible to internal teams across multiple functional areas, including the folks in the physical locations and the call center. For guests opting into the platform, on-board staff could find their specific location on the ship so their drink could get to them where they were if they had moved or to offer a complementary service if they were having issues with the entertainment systems in the room. Integration of the ship's on-board technology with the automation of back office process gave business operations teams the capacity to personalize more of the interactions with a guest and handle more cases because the systems were using real-time data to suggest next best actions and minimized their time on the phone resolving issues.

# Data and Computation

Design, and with it, experience, isn't just about making something that is beautiful to look at or pleasurable to use. Although those aspects are important, a higher purpose for design is to achieve market relevance and outcomes that are meaningful for people and society. In his book *How to Speak Machine: Computational Thinking for the Rest of Us,* my friend John Maeda explores this important distinction and the different types of design.[4]

## There Are Three Types of Design

- Classical design – activities which pertain to the design of objects we use in the physical world
- Design thinking – activities that enable companies to put the user at the center of every design decision and to create innovative products focused on human wants and needs
- Computational design – activities involving processors, sensors, memories, actuators, data, and networks

Today, some companies use classical design in the creation of physical products, and most use some form of design thinking similar to what we shared earlier to evolve products and services, but very few have even come near the space of computational design. The critical distinction between classical design versus design thinking and computational design is that the latter two have iteration built into their approaches.

In the context of a rapidly changing world, the idea that "timely design is more important than timeless design" is important. It's the philosophy of shipping an incomplete product followed by as many revisions as possible, instead of trying to ship a product that's complete. The deeper you get into creating digital products, the more fundamental this idea becomes to your ability to remain competitive.

The challenge for our established clients today is how do they get the system to move more in line with the rate of change? From a method perspective, one of the most critical steps is to create a virtuous cycle of data capture, integration, improvement, and implementation. This is as much about how you design your products, services, and processes to capture data as it is about having the culture to use it. Unfortunately, for most established companies, data exists, but the organization isn't built to design for it or create the reinforcing loop to use it to improve existing products and services or identify new ones.[5]

To incorporate design thinking into your business, data is a massive accelerant and important, but there have been many times where design thinking can be applied in companies with fragmented data infrastructure, although much less effectively. To operate at a level of computational design, however, a cohesive data infrastructure is required.

Interestingly, one of the best comparisons to understand this point is from two of the strongest digitally native companies: Netflix and Amazon. Think about your experience using Netflix versus Amazon Prime Video. From search functionality to content recommendations to navigation, the Netflix design is far ahead that of Amazon Prime Video. Much of this can be attributed to how their teams use qualitative and quantitative data to improve the user experience (UX).

One part of the Netflix functionality that is most well known is the use of data for recommendations. The Netflix recommendation engine uses algorithms to predict what shows you are likely to enjoy based on the behavior of other users who enjoy similar content. From a UX perspective, Netflix uses data trends to understand user behavior, identify patterns, and help prioritize where to focus its UX improvements. It then uses A/B testing to test those ideas with customers before scaling them to the 180M+ subscribers globally. An example is the ability to go directly from one episode to the next, which was only added once Netflix saw that pattern of behavior surface in the data. This virtuous cycle is only possible with the combination of a thoughtfully designed data strategy and the culture and ways of working that feed data and customer insights back into other capability areas in the business.[6]

Another avenue for capturing data is instrumentation. Take, for example, the cruise ship mentioned earlier. Instrumentation allows you to collect information on not just your digital products, but physical as well. As we dive into computational design, you can see how this can be incorporated into the design of original products.

The second advancement accelerating product and service design is computation. Today, much of product and service design relies on intuition and experience to solve design problems, but that is also starting to change. The combination of increasing processing power, data, and 3D modeling and visualization tools has created the ability to make and test designs that were not possible before. What computation allows you to do is replace the intuitive aspect of design with the ability to test hypotheses using computation to produce hundreds or thousands of design permutations to find multiple solutions.

An interesting example of how a product uses computation is the iPhone 11 and iPhone 12 cameras. They have computation built into every picture. When a user takes a picture, the camera captures eight pictures and then uses computation to compare and combine them to create the best shot. Using a combination of processors and machine-learning techniques, Apple has created a process called "deep fusion," or what Apple Senior Vice President of Worldwide Marketing Phil Schiller called "computational photography mad science."

## Computational Design

In 2015, the Dutch design firm Joris Laarman Lab and Dutch technology start-up MX3D started the design phase for Amsterdam's first robot-printed steel bridge – see Figures 8.4 and 8.5. As part of the design process, structural engineers from the engineering firm Arup

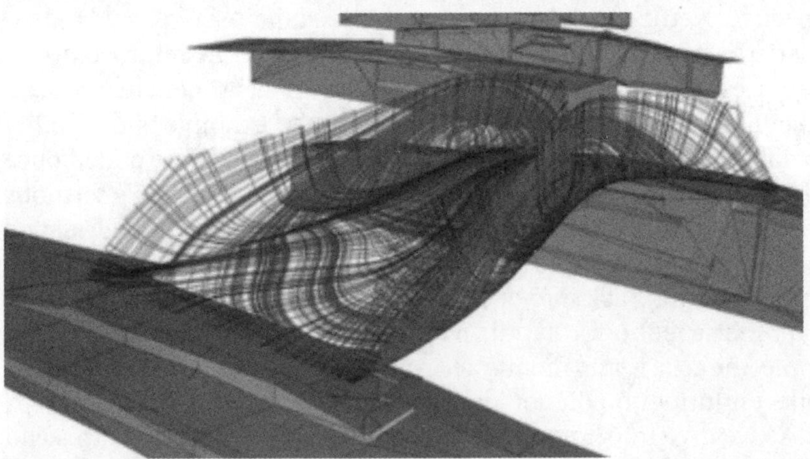

**FIGURE 8.4** Parametric design modeling for Amsterdam Bridge *Source: Joris Laarman Lab, MX3D; ©Arup*

**FIGURE 8.5** World's first 3D-printed metal bridge *Source: Joris Laarman Lab, MX3D; ©Arup*

used advanced parametric design modeling and generative algorithms to explore new shapes for the new bridge using code. Unlike with traditional design where the designer (or engineer in this case) would create multiple iterations themselves, with parametric design modeling, they could use software tools (in this case Grasshopper and Karamba and 3D modeling tool Rhino) to design a rough shape, lock in the components in the system, and then use code to tell the system what they want to optimize for. The software then uses generative algorithms to create successive iterations and ultimately land on the optimal final shape.[7]

What's powerful about this kind of design is that it can use computation to not just provide aesthetic options, but can incorporate material properties as well. This allowed the team to do load path analysis before the bridge was physically built. Through the code, the team could teach the algorithm which parts of the bridge were less critical, so the optimal design would also remove any excess material. When the design was locked, MX3D created intelligent software that transformed welding machines into 3D printing robots to produce a fully functional steel bridge.

The bridge was also instrumented with a sensor network that gathers data that will be used to build a digital twin to continuously monitor the health of the bridge under different environmental conditions. This will allow that virtuous feedback loop of data into the maintenance and evolution of the bridge.

Now, for some of you reading, this may feel like a look into the distant future, but the reality is that as Moore's Law continues to advance technology, data, and computing power at an exponential rate, it will enable new levels of computation that were previously impossible. Think about what computational design could do for the creation of new cars, sustainable packaging options, or digital service offerings. As leaders of businesses, this will not only impact the rate of your competitive offer development, but, importantly, how you think about skilling your people.

More important is the reality that the digitally native companies are already applying computation to their products, services, and experiences. For established companies thinking about how they want to compete, choosing to create a system that enables consistent, iterative gains for your products and services can be equally if not more impactful than setting out to create the next iPhone. Although, the best experience design organizations will be built for both. In an environment where change is accelerating, the value is not just in the outcome but the process to get there. Your experience capability will not only change what you can produce, but how fast you produce and evolve it and bring you ever closer to the aspiration of who you can be as a company.

## What Makes a Great Experience? LEAD (Light, Ethical, Accessible, Dataful)

In some ways we have to approach computational design as a new medium. Just as you can't judge a painting in the same way you'd judge a sculpture, you shouldn't assume the quality of computational design is determined by the same traits as traditional digital experience.

A great experience in the world of computation is Light, Ethical, Accessible, and Dataful (LEAD). Light reflects the idea of speed. In today's world, everyone wants everything to be fast and seamless. Though literal speed is one component, so is how quickly the user can navigate to get to the desired outcome. Have you designed an experience that aligns with the customer's expectations, or is there a level of friction that's deterring the engagement?

Ethical is an idea that's very important, but also constantly evolving. First is an idea that has been core for established brands for a long time: trust. Is the experience trustworthy? Does the user feel the experience and content being presented are transparent? But, also, are you handling my data in an ethical way? Data is a critical component to how this entire system works, but it also comes with the weight of responsibility.

Accessible addresses how easy it was to interact within the experience. Can I easily find what I need? Is the language clear? Has the design considered people needing special accommodation or needs?

Finally, Dataful addresses how you are using data to provide value. Is the user getting useful data throughout their experience? How have you used data to create a personalized experience?

LEAD creates a barometer that can be used to determine whether the experiences you are building are of quality to the end consumer, and it does so through the lens of computation.

As the world becomes increasingly digital, understanding how experience is evolving and adapting itself is critical. Though most companies today may not be ready for computational design, many digitally native companies are already moving in this direction. Part of the intent of sharing this broad perspective on experience is to help you start to visualize not only what your counterparts are doing, but what is possible and may be more commonplace in the future. With a clearer vision across all these dimensions of experience, you can start to map out where you need to go as a business and how to get there.

### DBT Takeaway: Experience

Sometimes, established businesses will see that their need to transform is evident, but they miss that it is not just about becoming more digital, or even about improving the customer experience. By this stage in the book, I hope you will have accepted the premise that digital business transformation is, in essence, business transformation for the digital age: a holistic approach to the way an organization thinks, organizes, operates, and behaves. Viewed through the lens of your experience capability, this means recognizing that every aspect of your business – whether customer-facing or internal – shapes the customer experience, and that your experience capability plays a central role in optimizing every component of the customer experience.

There are a few principles to live by when constructing your experience capability:

- Consider whether "experience" in your organization is truly multidisciplinary, with teams encompassing not just "experience" capability, but strategy, engineering, data, and product as well.
- Make sure your goal for experience capability is not only to change what you can produce, but how fast you are able to produce and evolve it. The "move fast" organizational goal is born out of the strategy, engineering, and data capabilities as well, but how you approach experience and design will prove pivotal to goal achievement.
- How will you build a system capable of moving at the rapid rate of change in the world? The key difference between classical design versus design thinking and computational design is iteration and continual improvement built on data, data systems, AI, and machine learning.

# CHAPTER 9

# Engineering

*"The real sources of advantage are to be found in management's ability to consolidate corporatewide technologies and production skills into competencies that empower individual businesses to adapt quickly to changing opportunities."*

Sources of advantage? Check. Creating technological competency? Check. Enabling your business(es) to adapt quickly to change? Check. This statement sounds like it could be part of a digital business transformation playbook of today. It was actually written by C.K. Prahalad and Gary Hamel in 1990 in their seminal *Harvard Business Review* article, "The Core Competence of the Corporation," six months before Sapient was founded.[1]

Prahalad and Hamel argued that core competency was the combination of skills that created competitive differentiation and advantage for a corporation. Core competencies had to fulfill three criteria:

- Provide potential access to a wide variety of markets.
- Make a significant contribution to perceived customer benefits of the end product.
- Be difficult for competitors to imitate.

What's even more interesting is that, in 1990, they made the connection that for technology to be part of a core competency, it had to directly connect to the creation of value.

So, if we have seen the need to connect technology to value for decades, and the need to make it part of the core competency of established corporations, why is it so challenging to do that today? Part of the reason is that established companies have been around for decades, many before enterprise IT even existed. They've been through different leaders and technologies, and their tech stack and capability reflect that journey. Add to that the massive on-premises technology and enterprise software investments made in the 1980s and 1990s and it becomes very hard to make a change. In January 2020, for example, we had a large client ask for help finding a COBOL developer, a language invented in the 1960s for mainframe computers. The presence of legacy technology is still very real.

Beyond legacy hardware and software choices, what's fundamentally different from 1990 is, as much as one could argue the connection between technology and value creation, most companies saw tech investment as primarily a risk and cost play. As the world came online, it inched closer to driving growth, but it often did so tangentially. It was never truly part of the core competency on which companies based their differentiation.

## Technology as a Cost Center to Technology as a Value-driver

There is growing recognition among businesses today that technology can create value to the customer and real differentiation around a company's product and service. This deep potential for value creation has shifted our understanding of technology as something that is ancillary to the business to something that is the lifeblood of the business. An example is being able to buy an airline ticket online, which in the old days was about risk and cost; you could buy it cheap on the online platform, and keep the cost low. Today, airline technology has advanced, allowing you to watch your on-screen entertainment on your own devices as opposed to onboard. In fact, you're seeing planes that don't have screens anymore: They've just got infrastructure that allows you to stream content onto your own devices. The boarding passes and the ability to select your seats are all examples of digital products. It is significant that airlines today make much of their money through allowing you to choose digital products.

Organizations that have historically considered risk and cost, and invest enough in technology to keep the risk at bay, have never really thought about it in the context of value, differentiation, and revenue generation. Airline seat selection is a good example; the idea was founded on faster check-in times and shorter call center queues as measures of risk and cost. In fact, it turns out that seat selection is now the second biggest generator of revenues for many major airlines.

Some mainframe computers built in the 1960s, 70s, and 80s haven't been touched in a long time because they're too expensive and too core. They engender the mindset that the risk and cost of replacing them is just too great and a process of papering over the spaghetti ensues. A bank, for instance, may have hard-coded everything into the mainframe computer and the legacy of that is the mainframe has hard-coded into it everything about how the bank used to do business. The process by which the bank runs was built into that technology, but not built into it in a way that allowed it to change, scale, or evolve.

Some of the key choices companies historically made were concerned with the extent to which they wanted to own and manage their technology infrastructure versus outsource it to a third party to manage. As cloud-based solutions have started to grow, it is very easy to continue the thinking of how can this new technology make existing parts of my tech stack more efficient and effective? Though this is certainly an understandable question, it also frames your view on how to leverage technology in the same way leaders approached it decades before.

Leveraging technology to create value for customers, on the other hand, requires a completely different set of considerations and orientation to how you think about building it. Naturally, technology silos tend not to exist in companies where the entire business operates with a digital mindset. Amazon is a company built latterly in a more digital world. Its technology does not belong to any particular group. Functionally every group can say, "Here's what I want to do in terms of service," but it's built as a complete picture. Amazon's technology is its product, the thing that is its biggest differentiator. That means it is oriented differently.

# Spaghetti Tech: The Layers of Enterprise IT

Because technology was not seen as a core competency, most established companies saw its value purely in the functionality that it delivered. For instance, if you were a bank, your business case was signed off based on the functionality that the specific technology project gave the company. There was no value to the capability itself. Today, the seminal shift in technology is now ingrained with the human experience. Your technology capability is key to how you create value for customers and your ability to remain competitive.

Shifting technology from being primarily functional to value-producing in established businesses is challenging because part of the process involves navigating the spaghetti-like architecture that has been built over decades. In the product chapter we talked about technical debt created by shortcuts in coding. Legacy architecture takes this to a whole other level: the layers that exist include data, hardware, software, and business processes. Because most of our clients have existed for more than 30 years, some more than 100 years, exploring their enterprise architecture is like taking a walk through the evolution of enterprise IT itself.

# Moore's Law

Over the past several decades, the vast majority of established organizations have been focused on digitizing their business: taking processes and using technology to make them more efficient. In turn, their technology and talent reflect that. Technology teams are often large, hierarchical, and made up of individuals with deep expertise in a particular hardware, software, or programming language.

In that same time, Moore's Law predicted that the number of transistors on a microchip would double every two years while the cost of computers would be cut in half in that same time. These ideas are illustrated in Figures 9.1 and 9.2. Basically, computers became smaller, faster, and cheaper as storage capacity increased. What we only imagined doing years before became not only possible, but affordable. This created fertile ground to rethink enterprise technology architecture and the role of technology in the enterprise.

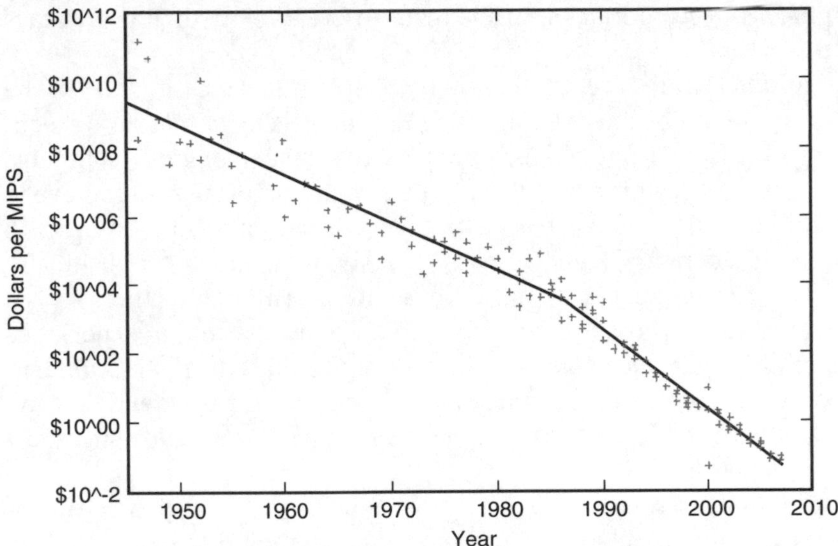


**FIGURE 9.1** Cost of computing

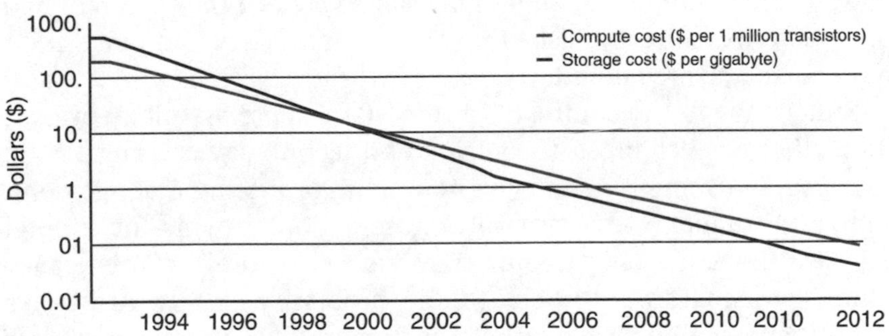


**FIGURE 9.2** Moore's Law – cost of storage

# Legacy Technology

As we have seen, "legacy", in the context of technology is a polite way of saying "out of date" or worse, "not fit for purpose." The technological skeletons of established companies include multiple architectures from point-to-point connecting mainframes, services-oriented architecture associated with middleware, to the client-server architectures built in the midst of the dot-com days. The combination of all of these creates a spaghetti-like architecture that technologists and engineers need to be able to navigate to create new digital products and services.

Add to that the fact that, to many people, the word "digital" in the context of their business has implied the advertising or marketing technology stack and front-end technologies. In a consumer goods company, for example, they may ask "What does a manufacturing system have to do with digital?" and come up with the answer "not much" – at least in theory. If you're in a bank, "digital" is taken to mean your website and your mobile app that is all of the front end of your architecture.

The same customer-centric dynamic we saw play out in experience is equally applicable to engineering; there should be no distinction between your front end or middleware relative to your back end. Yet too often we see that the back end is where mainframe and real legacy technologies live.

Companies used to have a website back in the day where customers would be able to go and place an order, and the order would essentially be a simple form. That form, at the back end, would spit out into a printer and someone would take the paper and start running around because an ecommerce order had just come through. It was the same person handling the order in the same way as if the customer had walked into the store and asked for the product. They had taken their front end and layered it on top of their existing processes.

Today, though the contrast is not as stark, there are many organizations that have changed their front-end technology and have good apps but the inventory management system, or pricing management, or property management system or reservation systems for a hotel chain are the same old systems they have had forever. This legacy technology jeopardizes the end-to-end process, which in turn risks negatively impacting the experience customers have with the business.

## The Impact of Product and Rise of Engineering

When digital was still a tangential idea, it was much easier to argue that technology's role was to support the *real* core competencies of a business. When digital started to disrupt the nature of competition itself for established businesses, the role of technology had to change. The easiest way to think about this shift is to look at how companies are categorized in the market. For established companies, P&G is a consumer products company, Marriott is a hotel chain, and Walmart is a retailer. Yet, Dollar Shave Club, Airbnb, and Amazon are all tech companies. Where established companies are classified by industry, digital natives are classified by competency. Digital companies aren't judged by the industries they disrupt but by their ability to use digital to create new products, services, and markets. In order to do that, technology could not just be a matter of delivering on an idea. Instead, digital companies hired engineers who could apply the possibilities of technology to solve problems.

Doing this as a start-up is much less complex than doing it in an established business. For an established business, not only do you have to address the technical debt built up over decades, but your transformation also requires that you disrupt the core competencies that created your successful differentiation to begin with. We've already talked about inserting strategists, product managers, and experience designers into shaping your value streams. Add engineers and you can feel the change that's afoot.

Our clients making this shift face a number of hurdles along the way:

- How do I associate engineering transformation to business and/or customer value to get sustained funding?
- How do I turn my legacy systems into value generators within my digital transformation?
- How do I divert more of my legacy run spend to growth and transformation?
- I am running Agile events, but how do I achieve real engineering agility?
- How do I achieve speed to market without taking unnecessary risk with resilience and stability?
- How do I generate value from the cloud instead of it being another data center?
- How do I connect modern engineering to customer-centric value?
- How do I know all of the investment I have made in modern technologies and techniques is working?

# Technology and Engineering

A 2019 study by *Harvard Business Review* found that the primary reason transformations fail is the inability of companies to scale digital innovations beyond pilots.[2] This is where established companies hit the wall created by traditional enterprise IT. They are working with a capability designed to make traditional core competencies more efficient versus those designed to fuel a new core competency.

From an engineering perspective, creating a core competency in digital requires lenses across three areas:

- Architecture
- Ways of working
- Talent

This means being able to effect change on front-stage and back-stage processes, including internal operations, as seen in Figure 9.3. Take, for example, the banking case from Chapter 7. For a bank setting out to improve the lending experience, it had to not only address the front-stage experience in branches or online, but also make the internal approach to processing loans more efficient. This starts to touch on the role of DevOps: Scaling change needs innovation tightly coupled with operations.

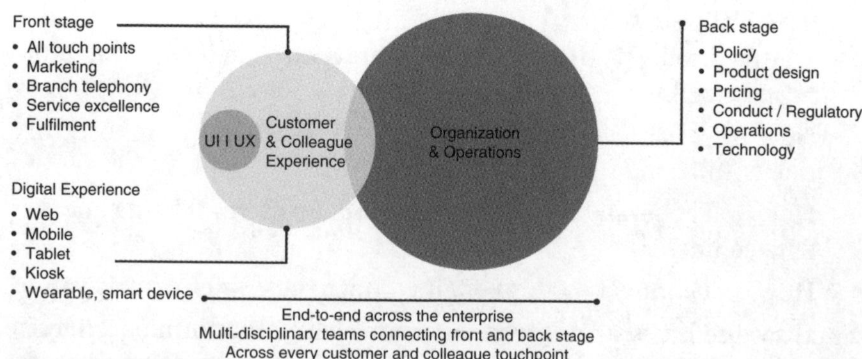


**FIGURE 9.3** End-to-end transformation

# Architecture: Cloud

One of the biggest challenges and opportunities that surfaced over the past decade is the rise of enterprise cloud. Over the course of this chapter what you won't see is a perspective on which tech trend is going to disrupt the enterprise space. This chapter, in fact this entire book, is focused on how to create the structures to power an agile, digital business. Cloud is different in that it's not a specific type of software, but a key design component for how you create flexibility and agility within your systems architecture.

As you saw earlier, one of the common questions clients ask is how to generate value out of cloud so it's not just another data center. In order to do that you have to understand what you are designing your overall architecture to solve and how you are creating value in that context.

If you are approaching cloud offerings as an alternative to components of your existing operational tech stacks, what you will get from it will primarily be efficiency. And, in some cases, that's where our clients choose to start, in order to get the business more comfortable with this way of working.

If you want to see the levels of value you keep hearing about from digitally native companies, you have to have a clear vision for how you are leveraging cloud-based services in the context of the products you are creating and the value streams within them. This is why digital business transformation cannot be done through technology alone. To create value requires an approach where all capabilities are working continuously in concert.

Cloud is fundamentally different from legacy architectures because it is decentralized, offering infrastructure platforms, services, and tools through the Internet. The options for cloud services are growing significantly. Gartner is predicting roughly a 17% CAGR in public cloud service revenue from 2018 to 2022.[3] Today, Amazon Web Services, Google, Microsoft Azure, Salesforce, and IBM lead cloud services. Your ability to wield the power of cloud requires understanding how it fits in your overall architecture and your decision making as you think about transforming.

From an architecture perspective, there are three main types of cloud service: Infrastructure as a Service (IaaS), Platform as a Service (PaaS), and Software as a Service (SaaS). IaaS offers on-demand access to help scale hardware, things like networking, storage, and servers.

PaaS gives you a cloud-based environment for testing and development where you can develop, manage, and host applications. Finally, SaaS gives you access to cloud-based software that you can access independently via the web or application programming interface (API) into your existing architecture. An example of SaaS that has gained increasing popularity is Communications as a Service (CaaS), which facilitates business communications through things like Voice over IP (VoIP), Internet telephone solutions, and video conferencing.

One of the biggest concerns for established companies considering cloud is security, so providers offer some combination of the following to address that: private cloud, public cloud, and hybrid cloud. Private cloud allows companies to host on their own data center and manage it themselves. Think of this as creating your own intranet with your cloud architecture protected by your own firewall and security. Public cloud is the opposite, where you are given access to the provider's environment and they manage the environment, infrastructure, and security for you. Hybrid is just that: a mix between the two where you determine what aspects of your environment you want to be public or private and determine the associated security and APIs to make the architecture work. The mix of providers across each of these segments continues to grow. It's important you know what role they play in your digital business transformation.

Cloud architecture and applications are part of the toolkit of a digitally native company, and like everything, your application of cloud will evolve over time based on the needs of your customers and business, the value streams you are activating, and the growth you seek to achieve. What cloud offers more so than its legacy predecessors is the flexibility to adapt with much greater speed than ever before.

## Microservices

The way in which applications are built is fundamentally changing. In traditional app development, any update, big or small, required a wholesale version update that impacted the work of every associated team. When you are operating a continuous release cycle, this approach has significantly detrimental impacts on speed, quality, and flexibility.

Instead of this monolithic approach, today many development teams are turning to microservices as an alternative.

Microservices is an architectural approach to building applications that partitions apps into services that can be built, tested, and updated independently of other services supporting the application. What this means is if you are building a banking app, for instance, your search and deposit functions would be managed as separate services that are loosely coupled through APIs. So, you could update either without impacting the development cycle of the other. This allows continuous development across services and also gives development teams enough independence to more quickly incorporate new innovations, features, or changing customer needs as well as to choose the tools most relevant to their service area. It also means that if you experience a failure in one service area, it doesn't take down the entire app.

The structure of microservices starts to touch on team structures and roles. When you shift to developing multiple microservices concurrently, you team sizes get smaller, but you may also have more developers working on the same app. You will also see how the flexibility it creates in terms of tools reinforces the need for an engineering role that can see across the entire system and, importantly, can architect the systems to work effectively.

One side advantage of microservices is that in the context of DevOps it starts to create real code artistry. Developers not only write code, but manage that code in a model of continuous improvement and integration. This creates a higher level of performance in the code itself and a different orientation: Not only are you going to build the house you're going to live in, you will be responsible for continuously improving it.

Similar to the evolutions we saw in legacy enterprise IT, companies are creating software specifically designed for these ways of working. In 2002, two Australians, Mike Cannon-Brookes and Scott Farquhar, created what would become the largest tech company in Australia: Atlassian. Atlassian built a suite of tools aimed at enabling Agile and Lean development teams, focused on improving software development, project management, collaboration, and code quality. What's interesting about Atlassian is it is geared toward creating a better experience for developers in an environment of continuous development versus primarily focusing on the experience of the project manager.

# Ways of Working: Agile, Lean, DevOps

The measures of value, speed, and quality applied to a successful product capability also anchor engineering. However, most traditional enterprise IT is still managed around time, scope, and cost and run through waterfall processes where budgeting is structured around a finite start and finish.

Shifting your technology function to a product and value orientation through the use of Agile, Lean, and DevOps amounts to significant changes in the way this capability operates:

- *The level of ambiguity in the work increases.* You need not just technologists, but engineers who can design how multiple technologies are applied from front stage to back stage to enable a product or service.
- *Teams have to be much closer to the customer.* To create valuable products, services, and experiences, your engineers have to know customer pain points and have visibility into feedback loops that they can relay to your technology teams.
- *Teams get smaller and more autonomous.* The multi-disciplinary teams designing the product or shaping the code, the nature of cloud-based technology, and shorter deployment cycles necessitate smaller teams that leverage experts.
- *Delivery will be continuous and delivery cycles will be shorter.* Code will be moving into production on a constant basis in order to build speed and quality and enable an environment of test and learn.
- *DevOps will be critical to creating end-to-end products and services.* DevOps helps to close the gap between your development teams and your existing IT operations architecture.

## Low Code/No Code

Another topic that has surfaced in client conversations recently is around Low Code and No Code application development. While they are often conflated, they address two different application development options. Low code is a type of application that helps professional developers develop applications with little hand-coding, essentially streamlining their work and helping accelerate the development process. No code, on the other hand, is geared toward "citizen developers," business users who do not know how to code, and allowing them to build apps through interfaces that don't require them to write any code at all.

Clients want to understand the implications of both to their businesses. Does this mean your customer apps can now be created much faster and by a broader set of people in your organization? No. You will not be building Uber off No Code applications.

In fact, Low Code and No Code have been around forever. When Visual Basic and WYSIWYG came out, they were essentially attempting to do the same thing, allowing internal business teams to build their own apps, thus putting less demand on IT operations. What Low Code and No Code are doing today is prioritizing the focus of your engineering resource and familiarizing more people with creating applications, rather than just being users.

As technology advances, this is likely the way the world will head, with a broader set of individuals having access to tools to develop their own apps. 15 years ago, you wouldn't have imagined the free website builder Wix. Tools will evolve, and what once required the skills of a large team of developers will one day take far fewer. While these tools won't be replacing engineers with business analysts any time soon, they do provide a window into the future and an opportunity to get your teams familiar with this way of working.

## Engineers

As mentioned before, the single biggest shift in the role of technology within established businesses is going from an efficiency play to value-creation. As you start to move into the space of product development, how you apply technology becomes less defined. It's less about creating an ecommerce site and more about creating an experience that will meet the needs of customers (and drive greater conversion). This could be across multiple channels using a variety of technologies and languages. This is where the engineer comes in.

Engineers follow a different profile than traditional technologists. They are polyglots, traversing multiple languages. The role they play is in identifying and activating what's possible through technology and testing and refining based on the needs of the customer. This is also why they will need to be in much closer proximity to the customer, and to the feedback loop from the customer, than ever before.

## Automation

In addition to how software development is managed, automation is changing how it's done. Continuous development requires continuous feedback loops. We often think about analytics and automation in the context of understanding the customer, but they are equally critical in the context of engineering and software development, and specifically DevOps. Think about the measures of speed and quality in the context of development and release cycles. One of the most common questions our clients ask is "How do I achieve speed to market without taking unnecessary risk with resilience and stability?" Part of the answer to this question lies in updating the software development process itself.

Today, software is updated through continuous releases. Software test-automation allows the developer to automate this process, testing whether the new application will work with the other systems and applications it needs to interface with. Yet, in a study of software testers and mobile developers from mid- and large-size organizations, 73% said they run at least 100 tests prior to each software release and 76% said they test the majority of their code manually. Now, think about developing software in that spaghetti architecture from earlier and you can start to see how this approach might eat away at those key metrics. As the pace of development and releases accelerates, automation will play a key role in producing value with speed and quality.[4]

## It's All About the Talent

If you step back and think about building a digital capability – your digital moat – it will not work without the right engineering and technology talent. This chapter presented a need for fundamentally different talent. It requires finding engineers, in addition to technologists, and then building teams that can execute in this new paradigm.

Let's start with the engineers. A great engineer is hard to find. Plain and simple. While there are many strong technologists with deep expertise in specific software, being able to problem solve in an ambiguous context and lead Agile and Lean technology teams is a different skillset. We talked about engineers being polyglots, working across multiple languages, but they also have to work across technologies. What's interesting is that some of what attracts engineers to companies is similar to the shift in the nature of the work itself. They want to know, "Do I want to solve these problems for you, with these people?"

As you think about developing your engineering talent internally, it will also require a different approach than would be the case for a specialist. In the past you could develop Java expertise in three to four years. To develop the polyglot-like skillset of an engineer requires closer to eight to ten years to allow them to experience multiple technology cycles and evolutions.

Building up a strong team of developers is also key. We are already seeing the demand for software developers skyrocket. The US Bureau of Labor Statistics predicted the demand for software developers to grow 22% from 2019 to 2029. This is relative to 4% for all occupations.[5] What's also interesting is that within specific technology areas, your talent may profile differently. Technologists working in cloud will need to be able to work with a certain level of independence since they won't have the same infrastructure support as, say, a Java developer. They need to not only know their code, but also understand infrastructure and be able to deploy that code on their own. Similarly, technologists working on AI and machine learning have to have a strong understanding of data.

If you consider the combination of problem solving across multiple languages and technologies combined with automation, you start to see the need to upskill your existing talent to new ways of working that will make your organization both relevant and adaptable. And, though it is daunting to think about how to access the talent and drive the change your business needs, there are multiple avenues to get you there. As we get into the "How" section of the book, we will explore those in detail. For now, it's important to remember that the transformation of your IT and engineering capability is key to making digital a core competency and to unlocking what's possible for you as a digital business.

## DBT Takeaway: Engineering

Today, technology is ingrained with the human experience, and so your organization needs to regard technology as the service, not something that is ancillary to the service. Your engineering capability is key to how you create value for customers and your ability to remain competitive through differentiation around product and service. In building it, here are the main considerations:

- Find and hire engineers to complement traditional technologists. Great engineers can and will identify and activate what's possible through technology based on the needs of the customer.
- Search and destroy any traditional technology silos. In leading organizations today, where the entire business is digital, technology silos tend not to exist.
- Eradicate any lingering belief in the business that technology is a cost center. Instead, see it for the potential it can create for the business.
- Determine whether an old-school risk and cost approach is leading your organization to paper over the messy, spaghetti code of back-end systems. It is? That's costing you more money and time and is perpetuating a problem that will need to be addressed when, inevitably, that system eventually falls over.
- Cloud matters. How can you match the levels of value derived by digitally native companies, by leveraging cloud-based services in the context of the products you are creating and the value streams within them?
- Shift to a microservices approach where apps services can be built, tested, and updated independently of each other. This will dramatically improve your speed, quality, and flexibility.
- How will you leverage automation for testing, so that software can be updated through continuous releases?

# CHAPTER 10

# Data

There has been an interesting, if seemingly paradoxical, trend happening across broadcast TV networks in the United States. The performance of new network programming has been lackluster, yet the cancellation rates for new shows has hit a 10-year low. Between 2014 and 2018, on average 54.4% of new shows were cancelled compared with 66.8% from 2009 to 2014. The trend continues when you look at all shows, both new and existing. Cancellation rates generally dropped by double digits between the 2017–2018 season and the 2018–2019 season.

In a world where streaming is lifting both the level of competition and expectations of content quality, it would be logical to expect these shows to get cancelled at even higher rates, rather than being renewed. But if you dig deeper, you can start to understand this trend.

In the past, same-day ratings were the barometer for a show's success. They determined audience as well as advertising. But things are starting to change. As networks build their own streaming platforms, ownership of content has become equally important. In conversations with *The Hollywood Reporter,* multiple network heads admitted that primetime schedules are just the starting point for their content, not the final destination. As they enter the streaming business, they need content to fuel their platforms.[1]

Owning content for your own platform makes sense, but what about the quality of that content? Why would the platforms hold on to shows that were not broadly successful from a ratings perspective in the first place, let alone choose to invest in them? Maybe their data were telling them something different. Or, maybe they were trying to pre-empt the same challenges that movie studios faced with the arrival of Netflix.

In 2013, Joris Evers, Netflix's director of corporate communications, told *The New York Times,* "There are 33 million different versions of Netflix." He was referring to its subscriber base at the time.[2] By 2020, that would become 183 million different versions. As its subscribers grew, Netflix's model of mass personalization, based on data and algorithms, uncovered audiences for long-tail, lesser-known content that fueled not only the market for niche and independent films, but the business model as well. The content cost less in licensing and, as Netflix had the ability to locate the unique audiences it would appeal to, it contributed to its ultimate success metric of retention, while continuing to feed its AI.

While identifying audiences who were interested in specific types of movies and shows helped Netflix determine the licensed content it wanted to bring into the platform, when it inverted these data, it became even more interesting. The company now had the ability to understand audience detail for specific movies: who saw it, where do they live, what else did they rent, and did they like it? It was a level of insight that movie studios never had and, importantly, could never provide to their advertisers. Now you could tell whether the audience watched the movie long enough to see your product placement and you had the data to identify that audience down to the individual level. For those long-tail movies, this gave Netflix the ability to estimate audience size using a similar algorithm to that used in its recommendation algorithm, and provided stronger negotiating power for licensing deals. Through the application of data, Netflix had created a superior relationship with the customer than the studios themselves.[3]

Then it found yet another use for the data: the creation of original content. Years before their rivals at the networks woke up to the fact, Netflix executives knew that content was what fed their platform and retained subscribers. In 2012, they bid more than $100 million to get first rights on the first two seasons of *House of Cards*. They hadn't seen a single scene. By using data to guide its decision making, Netflix could see explicitly that it had a ready audience that liked political thrillers, Kevin Spacey, and David Fincher; that it was a show which had had a successful run in a different country; *and* that the audience was sizable enough to warrant placing a bet on developing new content.[4] The rest, as they say, is history.

Netflix has now successfully expanded into original film and TV series. By the end of 2019, it had become the largest movie studio in Hollywood based on volume, doubling and in some cases tripling the output of its competitors.[5] The company's 2020 content budget was $18 billion, of which 50% was allocated to developing its own content. In a year when many studios and networks were postponing content creation due to the coronavirus pandemic, Netflix had already shot its 2020 slate of series and films and was working on the 2021 season. In July of 2020 alone, it introduced 59 original pieces of content from popular TV shows to new series, movies, documentaries, and anime.[6] Because it was not beholden to the studios for content, Netflix was also free from the constraints of release schedules, and the model has the agility to meet the unique needs of a streaming audience. Ultimately, the content feeds back into a system that uses data, AI, and machine learning to further develop an experience, products, and services that meet the needs of subscribers.

## Data as an Asset

In late June 2020, as the world was in the throes of the coronavirus pandemic and markets were volatile, something interesting happened. Netflix saw its market cap of $205 billion surpass that of Disney. Though COVID-19 certainly had an impact on Disney's business, even then the numbers don't seem to add up. Netflix is a company that has been around since 1997 and has $20 billion in revenue; Disney is an iconic brand almost 100 years old and with over three times the revenue, at $70 billion. Some might attribute their respective valuations to the tech bubble. Or something else could potentially be happening: The market is valuing the assets of these companies differently.

When you compare these numbers and think about the Netflix model just laid out, it provides one of the clearest pictures why, in this day and age, data is absolutely an asset. Disney's intangible assets in Q1 of 2020 were $100 billion alone. Its other major assets are vast content libraries, the Marvel catalogue, theme parks, studios, media networks, and their own streaming platform Disney+. By comparison, Netflix's major assets include some original content rights but are primarily its streaming platform and superior understanding of the customer.

What's interesting about looking at both of these businesses is, on the one hand, you have a platform business amassing a huge library. On the other, you have a business with a massive library building data and tech with the launch of Disney+. Because of the strength of the Disney content catalogue, they saw incredible growth in Disney+, adding almost 55 million subscribers in the first six months. And now, like Netflix, its success will depend on its ability to use data, experience, and a strong catalogue of content to retain those customers. In turn, Netflix is facing a formidable competitor with a diverse set of revenue streams and will need to navigate how it creates its own adjacencies that not only feed the current platform but drive growth for its business.

## Getting Started with Data

In a world where consumer behavior and preference are rapidly evolving, any company with the ability to understand and keep pace is incredibly valuable. A significant contributor to this sits in your data capability. And, let's be clear, there are multiple levels to this. You often hear people say the value of data is that it helps decision making, whether that is about the business or customers. Well, sure. But a data capability powered by AI and machine learning can actually make decisions for you, increasing the speed with which you execute your ability to personalize experiences for your customers, and freeing your teams up to focus on the next level of decisions that will drive more value from identifying adjacencies and new offerings. This is why data is a core component in the construction of your digital moat. It feeds every other capability area and enables the levels of computation introduced in the previous chapters.

Now, where to start? Like any other area of transformation, there are multiple paths that established businesses take in their data transformation. And, as with any journey, it's important to have a sense of what you want your final destination to be. In the case of data, that means asking yourself whether you see data as long-term assets or not. This will guide whether the incremental choices that you make along the way will get you to your desired destination.

Just like those TV executives and movie studio heads, established brands do not want to relinquish being the experts on their customers to digitally native competitors. And they certainly do not want to relinquish the customer relationship. In early 2020, we took a look at some of the common questions surfacing with clients across industries.

What you can see in the following questions is that, while everyone sees the opportunity for greater customer insights through data, most barely graze the surface of what it means operationally to be a data-driven company and how that influences an ability to move with speed and quality to create value.

**Customer Experience and Growth:**

- How could we "own" and holistically understand our consumers and start to get a handle on first-party consumer data?
- How can we stay more relevant in the eyes of our customers than our competitors?
- How can we effectively use our data to reach our customers and improve our experience?
- How can we personalize an interaction for a customer based on historical data?
- How can we harness the data we already have (and all the new data coming in from digital consumers) to drive growth?
- How can we access and provide real-time data on health and safety to our customers?

**Efficient Operations:**

- How do we harness our fulfillment data to improve efficiencies and spur innovation but fuel customer experience?
- How do we harness data to better manage everything from product assortments, business operations to consumer loyalty – and drive growth?
- How can we monetize our data while respecting customer privacy?

For established companies, the journey to become data-driven can be simplified into four lenses that can be applied across any aspect of your business, whether it's understanding your customers, your operations, or your people.

- **Utility:** How do you get useful data and analytics on the right audience (data sets and data architecture)?
- **Data Science and Artificial Intelligence:** How do you manage your data and create a closed loop system of automated learning and decision making?

- **Designing for Data:** How do you design your products, services, and experiences to collect data?
- **Ethics:** How does becoming data-led impact your ethical responsibility?

## Utility: How Do You Get Useful Data on the Right Audience?

For average Netflix users, the company has 60 to 90 seconds to grab their attention with compelling content before it loses them. In a business based on subscription fees, how it fills that 60 to 90 seconds is crucial. At one point, in the early days of Netflix's mail-in service, it used the star rating system to gauge what content a user was interested in, but today the data it collects on user viewing and search behavior include everything from how long users watch a program, the device they are viewing on, and the time of day they're watching. This data feeds 1,300 recommendation clusters that are incorporated into the handful of algorithms that make up the Netflix experience that a user interacts with on screen.[7]

The value of the Netflix data is its ability to fuel the AI the company uses for its user experience, to guide the content production, and to negotiate licensing deals. The data is structured in a way that allows Netflix to invert customer preference data to better understand the specific audience of a given movie. What is most powerful about the Netflix data strategy is that ultimately everything ladders back to the primary outcome of reducing churn and ensuring retention rates.

This ability to create data that can be accessed to optimize multiple business functions and offerings is the holy grail for many of our clients. From consumer products companies to pharmaceuticals, established companies across all industries are looking for ways to use data to drive a better customer experience, innovate new products and services, and run their operations more effectively.

Today, most established businesses have more data than they know what to do with. It's likely built up over decades and is optimized and siloed based on the initiative or functional area that it was designed to support. And, to no surprise to anyone, the primary users of those data can be very territorial about sharing it. It also tends to have more of a transactional orientation. In every major corporation you'll easily find data that rolls up to revenue and profit, but may find that the customer behavior data that feeds experience is either hard to find or gapped.

The components that shape any company's data strategy are the data sets, data architecture, and data science and AI that exist in its environment. Data sets give you a view into the data that currently exists in your business and the data you need to acquire to understand your target audience or business process. Data architecture is the systems and processes used to govern the types of data you collect, how it's used, stored, managed, and integrated. Finally, data science and AI create the algorithms that enable you to generate insights from your data and the computational ability to automate and evolve those insights. Within each of these areas are a plethora of approaches and disciplines that ultimately determine the value of your data assets.

## Data Sets: Do You Have the Data You Need to Understand Your Business and Customers?

What do you think those movie studios would give to have access to Netflix customer data? The answer to this question gets to the importance of your data set and the importance of creating a data set that gives visibility into the drivers of your outcomes. Today, most companies supplement their first-party, proprietary data with second- and third-party data sets, creating a mix of deterministic and probabilistic data. Deterministic is data you know to be true, which means it is known, factual data about a user. Probabilistic, on the other hand, is inferred based on patterns across similar data sets. This enables companies to get a more holistic view of the customer even though they may not have the mechanisms in place to capture these data themselves. What's powerful about a platform like Netflix is the amount of deterministic data they have available on their users. They know for a fact what you watch, what you search, where you pause. Meanwhile, their algorithms can create probabilistic assumptions on what content will resonate with you, that then becomes deterministic when and if you engage with that content. Very powerful stuff.

Unfortunately, most companies do not have that level of data on their customers and use the combination of data sets to address gaps and create a more holistic picture. We are also starting to see the rise of zero-party data. Unlike first-party data, zero-party data is any data that a customer proactively shares. This marries a customer's desire for personalization with a brand's ability to get their direct input on preferences (as opposed to inferring them based on behavioral data).

Ultimately, your data sets are important because they are what fuel your AI. Without the right, robust data, you won't have enough inputs to make the predictive components of your machine learning accurate or valuable.

## Data Architecture: Is the Data in a Format and Structure That Are Accessible?

If you've ever played the telephone game with cups and string as a kid, it can be not too dissimilar from the data architecture at large companies. In the past, every time a company wanted to connect the systems that housed their data, they had to do so as separate steps. Want to connect your customer relationship management (CRM) system with your data warehouse? That's one integration. How about your CRM to your demand-side platform (DSP)? Another integration. Numerous systems were connected one by one through individual data integration efforts.

People have been talking about a single view of the customer, data warehouses, and data lakes forever. In reality, this web of siloed data sources made creating a unified view of the customer very challenging. Systems were viewed in relation to the functionality they brought to a capability, not the value their connection could bring to a customer. As a result, they would progress at different speeds where one may be far ahead of the other and viewed as a massively expensive white elephant project. The reason why creating the unified view is hard is because you can only do it through the interconnection of these capabilities. In a closed-loop ecosystem, you can start to cater to all of these.

In 2010, a software engineer named Dave McCrory introduced the idea of data gravity. Similar to the law of gravity where objects are attracted to one another through gravitational pull, data gravity asserts that as data sets become larger and larger, they become harder to move.

As a result, the data is anchored in place and continues to grow. Meanwhile, things like applications and processing power are attracted to the data itself and move to where the data resides.[8]

Today, customer data platforms (CDPs) are being introduced as a central connection point for customer data coming from different systems. So, instead of connecting those systems individually, they each plug into a central source that can scale your customer data across your business through the cloud. In addition, the CDP creates a single identity for an individual. So, instead of having five distinct IDs for an individual in five systems, you would have one unified ID in your CDP that accesses data across the distinct systems. What this then allows you to do is understand where you're missing data for any given use case.

Think about the idea of creating a unified view of a customer and a unified customer experience. It simply wouldn't be possible without unified data that's accessible broadly. CDPs enable that for your customer experience and, once unified, can enable that for your operations as well. And, importantly, this is a major point of differentiation between established companies and leading digital businesses. Digitally native companies are created assuming data is an asset and a core capability, so not only is their data architecture designed from the beginning to unify their data but their business is designed to monetize it. The greater this divide becomes, the more dependence established companies will have on digital natives to understand their own customers. That's a pretty scary thought.

Today, cloud-based CDPs make the prospect of connecting your data architecture much more affordable. Though it may feel daunting to think about unifying your data, doing so is also foundational to your ability to create value in a digital world.

## Data Science and Artificial Intelligence

How do you manage your data and create a closed-loop system so your data capability is helping your business learn and make decisions in real time?

There's a theory that was developed in the mid-twentieth century to describe how an individual develops competence in a particular skill. It suggests that, when we learn, we go through four phases: unconscious incompetence (where you don't know what you don't know), conscious incompetence (where you are aware of what you don't know), conscious competence (where you have mastered something but it requires effort), and unconscious competence (where the skill has become second nature and you no longer have to think about it to do it well).

This is similar to how you can derive value out of your data capability. Your goal is not just understanding your customers or your business better. Your goal is to harness that capability to create better products, services, and experiences for your customers *and* identify new areas of opportunity for your business. A simple way to think about it is your data science team partners with your other capabilities to take your understanding of your customer in any given use case from unconscious incompetence to conscious competence. You then apply AI approaches, such as machine learning, to turn that into unconscious competence, which elevates your products, services, and experiences. This is similar to the development of the Netflix recommender algorithms: First, each algorithm had to be tested to vet the strength of its ability to predict relevant content; then it could be incorporated into the recommender systems to create a better experience for users and to ensure high retention rates; and, finally, through machine learning the company could perpetually learn from each user event through computation.

Though the focus often goes to the speed of automation through AI and machine learning, 80% of the time consumed in most AI and machine learning projects goes to data preparation and engineering.[9] This is why the notion of replacing human beings with AI is not a realistic one any time soon. However, the methods and tools those humans apply to preparing the data and designing the algorithms for AI will continue to evolve. Because of the proliferation of data and the steady increase in computational power, these algorithms can now be effectively applied to massive data sets and automated through machine learning. The application of AI and machine learning can then create the unconscious competence of your organization, enabling your machines to act, make decisions, and learn.

When you create this generative loop, where each capability reinforces the other, it allows your organization to move within your existing parameters at speed. And, because of automation and AI, it gives you the strategic inputs and frees up your teams to start exploring adjacencies and potential partnership opportunities to develop new products and services.

## Designing for Data: How Do You Design Your Products, Services, and Experiences to Collect Data?

So, we know that your data sets are what will fuel your AI capability. But creating the data sets you need is not always easy, or in some cases, the data is just not available in the format in which you need it. In the experience chapter, we talked about the role data and computation plays in experience design, but experience and product play a critical role in data as well. Though good experiences use data, great experiences use and gather data. This is why the relationship between the product team and data team is so critical. Product should connect your data and experience capabilities to ensure data collection is part of the design process so that you can create a mechanism to continue to feed your algorithms with more information. This creates a generative loop across your business that allows for constant learning and iteration.

## Ethics: How Does Becoming Data-led Impact Your Ethical Responsibility?

We exist in a world where companies are competing in a still relatively unchartered data environment. The benefits of personalization come with the responsibility to ethically govern how we create these experiences. With the exception of zero-party data, which is in the early stages of gaining traction, in most data situations the human beings that sit at the heart of our data still have limited insight or control over how their data gets used. In the context of our Netflix preferences, it can feel fairly innocuous, but what if Netflix uses your viewing patterns to target you with political ads? What about the phones and driverless cars that know where we are at any moment in time? Or the application of machine learning to our health and insurance? In reality, we are only beginning to understand and address the ethical implications of collecting all these data and ultimately using it for a purpose the customer has not knowingly allowed.

We are starting to see government and corporations lean in to establish guidelines on ethics for a digital world. The European Union (EU) developed principles for ethical AI, and so has the Institute of Electrical and Electronics Engineers (IEEE), Google, Microsoft, and others like the Organization for Economic Co-operation and Development (OECD), an intergovernmental organization that represents 37 countries, including the United States, United Kingdom, and Japan, in fostering policies to ensure equality, opportunity, and well-being across a number of socioeconomic areas.[10]

Though these are great steps forward, the complexity of creating ethical standards across a global environment is infinitely complex. This is where it's important that companies be thoughtful about ethically approaching data strategy as well as their digital strategy, in order to ensure alignment to your values as a company and to preserve the trust you've built with your customers and employees. As with any product, consumers want a clear exchange of value for their data. If they are giving you their information, how is that bettering their experience? This is where mutual value and ethics go hand in hand.

As we design products, services, and experiences for data, we can use a few simple principles to guide how we ensure we are doing so with an ethical lens:

1. Be clear about the value you provide the customer in exchange for their data.
2. Include data in your design so the customer can give you the data easily.
3. The data should only be used for the purpose the customer has agreed to – trust is everything.

While we've spoken about data from a product perspective, these questions are at the crux of data privacy debates from a marketing perspective. How do you differentiate between personalized marketing and being intrusive? These are all part of the ethical responsibilities that companies must weigh and plan for as they enter the digital space.

### DBT Takeaway: Data

The last, but not the least, of our SPEED capabilities is data. In the next section of this book, we explore organizational change, the components of successful digital business transformation, and what those transformation journeys might look like – being, or becoming, data-driven as an organization is one thread that runs through all of them.

We have seen already that one of things that leading digital businesses do well is to harness the power of data and AI to learn and refine their products and services. Your own shift must be to treat data as a key intangible asset, for your organization to build over time, and to optimize a data capability that will give you the same regenerative muscle as a digital native:

- Develop a data strategy, and the capability to serve it, that puts data to work to drive a better customer experience, innovate new products and services, and run your operations more effectively.
- Challenge your organization to be data-driven operationally and recognize how that increases your ability to move with speed and quality to create value.
- Remember that the ability to access connected data to optimize multiple business functions and offerings is the holy grail:
  - Consider carefully what data is useful to collect in order to understand your business and customers.
  - Consider how data is stored, managed, and integrated. Challenge your organization to unify its data in service of the single customer view and connected customer experience.
  - Consider how AI and machine learning can enable the "unconscious competence" of your organization, where the loop of making decisions, and learning, in real time becomes second nature.
- Good experiences use data, but great experiences use and gather data. Ensure that your experience and product capabilities are in service to your data capability, as well as vice versa.
- We are still in frontier land when it comes to data and ethics. As you build a data-led business, put yourself in the mindset of the people whose data you hold: It's not just what's legal, but what's ethical.

# CHAPTER 11

# Leading a Gryphon Organization

The primary drivers for digital business transformation are either significant opportunity or existential threat. The opportunity to reimagine the service and experience your organization offers, to increase relevance and revenue, will often feel like something that it can get to later. The case for digital business transformation in the face of existential threat is one that is far easier to make.

Many business leaders have been stung into action by the realization that the need to actively defend their position has taken on a new dimension: the threat of being superseded by an unseen, aggressive, and digitally oriented predator that comes from outside the historical competitive set. The predator metaphor is a useful one through which to understand the digital business transformation imperative.

In any ecosystem, its living things interact and evolve together; behaviors and hierarchy develop in a form that promotes equilibrium. In a business context, large and successful organizations have established themselves as a set of traditional apex predators, an ascent based on their decades, or even centuries, of expertise, evolution, and depth of capability within a defined industry sector. When a new predator arrives suddenly in this ecosystem, one that looks and behaves differently from anything seen before, it causes traditional predators to struggle because its sudden incursion stretches the limit of their comprehension and ability to react.

Where the Gryphon of legend was half lion, half eagle, and consequently dominant among all creatures, the business Gryphon is equipped with powerful hybrid capabilities, an original approach, and the ability to move freely across the Gryphon Zone. Gryphons are born every day. They disrupt our understanding of the world as it exists today, and instinctively break previously assumed boundaries to combine the best of technologies, services, and experiences. It would be incorrect to assume, however, that the speed, agility, and technological power that digital natives display mean the Gryphon Zone can be accessed by them alone.

The last several chapters have laid out the architecture for building the capabilities of a digital company, but there is still one final piece of the puzzle: the organization. To be a Gryphon organization is not about age or size, but about state of mind. It is here that the idea of the Gryphon has important parallels with the digital business transformation imperative. The leaders of companies exploring, or embarking upon, digital business transformation initiatives are effectively on a quest to transmute from traditional predator to Gryphon and to access the Gryphon Zone, which is the space and time that will allow them to defend and expand; to repel territorial incursions, certainly, but also to reimagine and reengineer their businesses for future success.

What follows are the behaviors and ways of working that you as a leader need to nurture in your people, whether you're leading a company of 50,000 or a team of five. How do you enable them to operate effectively in an environment that's constantly changing so that your business can build the muscle to do the same? Essentially, how do you lead a Gryphon organization?

## Learning to Think Differently

One of the biggest challenges established organizations face is that most companies are great at their core business, but not great at reimagining the future of their business. The reason those companies are stuck is not that they don't see the need for change, nor that they fail to see the imminent threat of disruptive competitors encircling them, but that entrenched beliefs and behaviors are holding them back from making the organizational change that is an essential part of digital business transformation.

Organizational change is hard. It's hard because it requires, first, the acceptance that digital business transformation necessarily goes beyond the surface and permeates all the way through an organization and, second, the commitment and resilience to get that done. To enable change at this enterprise level in turn requires leadership that can effectively embed it as a core capability; one that impacts everything from talent and hiring, to finance, to customer services, and, yes, to technology. And on a more personal level, it requires leadership that creates new bridges across organizational silos, getting teams to anchor to something bigger than the vertical relationships they've relied on. It requires leaders who think from an entirely different perspective about the purpose and nature of the organization and every aspect of the way it operates.

In their book *The Network Imperative: How to Survive and Grow in the Age of Digital Business Models*, Barry Libert, Megan Beck, and Jerry Wind write:

> *Thinking about things differently is surprisingly difficult. And it's even harder for people whose thinking and habits to date have created great success – leaders like you. The average CEO has 30 years of business experience on which she habitually relies . . . the neural pathways created in her brain by those years of experience run deep and feel reliable. But the world is a very different place now than it was even ten years ago. The same thinking, and the actions it drove, that led to market success in 2005, 1995 and 1985 are not likely to work now.*
>
> *Ask yourself this: how long has it been since you have examined your core beliefs and the related actions. For most of us this happens rarely, especially in business where industry practices rule the day.*[1]

The authors' solution to this intractable problem, where the core beliefs and default actions of the leaders charged with responsibility for transforming the business are a significant part of the challenge, is "inversion." The process of inversion is nothing less than deliberately and contrarily uninstalling everything you think you know about your business and industry and replacing those beliefs with their direct opposites.

To be able to invert everything you think you know about your industry or to reimagine the future of your business through the mindset of a disruptive new entrant will be the starting point of organizational change for your business and will immeasurably increase the chances of successful transformation.

# Characteristics of a Gryphon Organization

The power of the Gryphon is in the combination of features that enable it to move freely across a Gryphon Zone where traditional territorial demarcation is obsolete. Taken individually, each feature may look impressive but they're familiar. Taken together, they are unbeatable.

The Gryphon organization possesses similar strengths grounded in the unique combination of tangibles and intangibles that enable it to continuously create value in an ever-changing environment. What follows are the characteristics of a Gryphon organization based on my observations of leading digital companies that have entered market segments and successfully disrupted them, as well as of established businesses across various industry sectors that have shown they have what it takes to respond to, and even to become, the disruptive threat.

## Customer Obsession

In Chapter 4, I looked at the things that successful digital businesses do consistently well. The first four, of six, read like this:

- They have clarity on what need they are serving, what problem they are solving, and for whom. This clarity is powerful because it allows them to focus and be the company they were born to be.
- They understand value, and first of all, the value to the customer.
- In turn that value to the customer can be turned into value for the business.
- They focus on designing a great experience. In fact, these experiences tend to shape and reset customer expectations.

Do you see how often "customer" comes up and how core it is to the success of any Gryphon organization: youthful or established? Think about the large consumer packaged goods (CPG) company that connected the ideas of sustainability, purpose, and transformation to how they came to market. Customer obsession is about more than paying lip service to the idea that the "customer is king." It's more existential than that. Customer obsession is building your business around the belief that consumers and their rapid uptake of technology are the drivers of change, that the number one priority is how to create value for the customer, and that there is a world of competitors out there ready to pounce if you become complacent about what you do now versus what the shifting dynamics of consumer behaviors and emerging technology are telling you about what customer value will look like next.

We've already seen how product and service design has evolved from being about the "above the glass" experience to an approach which recognizes that what sits in the organization "below the glass" is just as important. How experience includes everything that touches a user of a system, and improves satisfaction and delight. How the goal is to surface, design, and build ideas that will unlock value, adopting a customer-centric view that permeates all the way through an organization.

Creating this connected customer-centric orientation means both your teams and systems are designed to identify and realize value for the customer, shifting away from the siloed approaches of data capture and execution of the past.

## Outside-in

The very nature of a Gryphon is that they are something "other"; they do not look, or behave, like a traditional predator and they do not feel constrained by the established boundaries, practices, and processes that define what is business as usual.

An outside-in approach is grounded in the idea of understanding how critical forces in the world will shape the customer experience and expectations and then harnessing those forces to create real outcomes. Why is it that digital natives define themselves as technology companies whereas established companies, whose business they are out to disrupt, define themselves by industry: a retailer, a hotel chain, or a bank? The difference is that digital companies are judged (and judge themselves) by how they use digital to serve a need, create new products and services, and – for businesses such as Amazon, Apple, and Google – to cut across traditional industry demarcations.

Outside-in is a customer-led perspective that allows an established business to break free of its constraints. That doesn't mean doing away with all that is good about a company even when the threat from digital disruptors feels the greatest. From near bankruptcy in 2004, Lego turned its then 70-year-old business around to be named Brand Finance's "Most Powerful Brand in the World" just a decade later. It reframed its business to encompass digital, content, and entertainment, and with renewed purpose delivered record profits. The outside-in perspective helps give established companies a vision of how things can be done differently and how to keep transforming and scaling the nature of their business. Today, we see clients in the hospitality space rethinking the role their hotels play in the communities they're part of, including how they can create new digital platforms that leverage consumer technology to change the landscape of hospitality.

What that translates to is breaking past the "not invented here" orthodoxies that block new ideas and ways of working from permeating the business. Instead, it embraces finding solutions across organizational silos as well as building partner ecosystems where your internal capability doesn't exist.

## A Willingness to Disrupt Yourself

Disruption is often associated with innovation, risk-taking, speed, agility, and a willingness to challenge the norms and disrupt the business itself in order to enter new markets and categories. These are all traits of smaller, younger digital businesses, for sure, and can be the first type we think of when we consider Gryphon organizations. Of course, some of those start-ups then scale up and become an Amazon, Apple, or Netflix: huge, successful companies that maintain a disruptive culture in everything they do.

Jeff Bezos's annual letters to Amazon shareholders often make worthwhile reading. In 2016, the Amazon founder and CEO outlined his now legendary "Day 1" philosophy. At the core of "Day 1" is the principle of always focusing on outcomes rather than outputs: on results, not processes. The idea of his company ever reaching "Day 2" is unthinkable. For Bezos, the generally larger and established "Day 2" organizations represent stasis where decisions are made, but made slowly and with an emphasis on whether the process was followed correctly rather than whether the intended outcome was achieved.

"The outside world can push you into Day 2 if you won't or can't embrace powerful trends quickly," wrote Bezos. "If you fight them, you're probably fighting the future. Embrace them and you have a tailwind."

It's a neat summation of what building a disruptive culture looks like: first, the acceptance that change is exponential and accelerating; second, that in order not to "fight the future," you have to build an organization that is restless, inquisitive, outward-facing, and in constant beta mode. Constant beta is that self-imposed regimen that values progression more highly than perfection. Progression builds belief; perfection (or at least an artificial sense of perfection) builds complacency.

The building of a disruptive culture is something that can, and arguably should, be done in iterative fashion. Herb Kelleher, co-founder and former CEO of Southwest Airlines – pioneer of the low-cost airline model that disrupted the industry – said, "Culture is what people do when no one is looking." He also said, "If you rest on your laurels, you'll get a thorn in your butt."[2] We can't all be like Herb, or even like Jeff. When building a company from Day 1, it's easier for a founder-CEO to steer the culture in the direction they want to go. When you're attempting to navigate a 100-year-old retailer through a storm of change, becoming a more disruptive organization entails identifying the products you want to improve and changing organizational structures and behaviors as you go.

Think about our banking example from the product chapter. For established organizations, disrupting yourself combines changing your orientation to the products and services you produce, alongside creating new systems and ways of working that can create that good disruption to help your organization move more nimbly.

Let's look at some of the blockers that a retail client had identified when Publicis Sapient began working with them in 2014:

- It was trying to fix digital channels individually, rather than focusing on customer experience across touchpoints, policies, and procedures.
- Digital strategy had developed independently from business strategy where it should have supported the overall group business strategy.
- The dual business and technology project structure was inefficient and slow. The retailer needed to "take digital and make it the change agent for the group rather than for the channel."

Through what was ostensibly a product-based customer journey entry point, the company began to shift not just the technology behind those products and services, but their culture, organization, and way of working. Crucially, it adopted many of the behaviors mentioned in this chapter, such as removing the silo mentality and emphasizing progression over perfection. By being willing to not just disrupt its capabilities, but also their ways of working, the retailer was able to start to create the orientation and adaptability of a Gryphon organization.

## Winning by Failing

In a now famous letter to shareholders in 2018, Amazon's Jeff Bezos wrote:

> *As a company grows, everything needs to scale, including the size of your failed experiments. If the size of your failures isn't growing, you're not going to be inventing at a size that can actually move the needle. Amazon will be experimenting at the right scale for a company of our size if we occasionally have multibillion-dollar failures. Of course, we won't undertake such experiments cavalierly. We will work hard to make them good bets, but not all good bets will ultimately pay out. This kind of large-scale risk taking is part of the service we as a large company can provide to our customers and to society. The good news for shareowners is that a single big winning bet can more than cover the cost of many losers.*[3]

He went on to point to the Fire phone as a failure, but which accelerated the rollout of Echo and Alexa in 2014. Since then, Alexa has grown in technological ability and reach, with the number of Alexa-powered devices "in the hundreds of millions," according to the company.

Amazon, like all good businesses, does everything it can not to fail. Everything, that is, apart from not trying, trying slowly, or thinking small. The chance of failure is just one it is willing to accept as it follows a product-management process that allows for a disruptive culture, for continuous improvement, for a test-and-learn approach. For would-be Gryphon organizations, putting this process in place is what matters. Failure is just an option, an occasional, necessary evil.

It is also the case that speed doesn't necessarily have to come at the expense of quality. Instead, successful digital businesses expect and plan to learn and to continuously improve on what they build.

Business leaders have realized that their company's success lies with how quickly and effectively they are able to navigate rapidly changing customer expectations and competitive disruption – something which Gryphons do instinctively, but that established businesses must retro-fit.

And that retrofit can be seen today across those companies that are adopting iterative approaches to improving customer experience. One of the world's largest quick-serve restaurants is doing this every day by taking the data it gathers from your mobile and drive-through activities to determine how to optimize those experiences more effectively.

The shift here is, as we've seen, from a historic focus on time, scope, and cost to focus instead on speed, i.e., how fast you can put an idea into the world. The shift is to how you do that with quality so that the risk of breaking things, while present, is minimized. The shift is to how you make sure you're not just meeting the scope of a project but delivering product of value to the customers and to the business.

When you make the shift to speed, quality, and value you gain the ability to move at the speed of disruptive change in the face of uncertainty. Essentially, you gain the ability to move at the speed of a Gryphon.

It's quite easy to read through these characteristics, nod your head, and move on. But here's the thing: for 99% of established companies, living these characteristics requires massive cultural and behavioral shifts. And guess what? Changing the way people behave is much more difficult than acquiring a new capability. Just like you, they've built careers off a set of behaviors that have made themselves and your company successful. They've built relationships and loyalties within the silos they've operated in. And, many will have built expertise that will need to evolve. That's a lot of change.

Leading through this change with clarity and empathy while role modeling the behaviors you want to create will require clarity of vision, commitment, and consistency. In the next chapter, we'll explore some components of successful transformations that can help you take those steps forward and help your people to do the same.

# SECTION 3

# HOW

# CHAPTER 12

# Components of Successful Digital Business Transformations

While there's no single path to successfully digitally transforming your business, over the years certain components have consistently produced better outcomes. In this chapter, we'll explore those tangible and intangible choices. The following 10 steps will keep you on track as you begin to elicit the organizational changes that will underpin your transformation journey.

## 1. Always Remember the Ultimate Goals of Digital Business Transformations (the DBT BHAGs)

When transforming large organizations, it can be very easy to get lost in the weeds of capability choices, personal agendas, and most of all, the real response of organizations and the people in them to resist change. So, step one is to remember that ultimately, you are setting out to do two things:

1. Creating an organization that can continually change at pace with the changes around it
2. Constructing the capability to identify and realize value for your customers and business through digital

As a leader, this orientation to what you are setting out to do, combined with the specific choices you make on the outcomes you want to drive, provides a frame for all the decisions you will make with your teams. It's not meant to be rigid because it will be constantly refined and tested, but the clarity of direction when making decisions will be one of the most powerful benefits you will provide to keep your teams and objectives connected.

## 2. Align the Team Around a Shared Vision

This takes us back to the Ignite activities of the PS How, gaining stakeholder alignment. One person cannot drive transformation alone. Whether it's the CEO or chairman of the board, it makes no difference. Aligning your core team is critical. At the end of the day, these are the leaders that the broader organization will look to for direction and guidance. If they are not bought in, their teams will prioritize the work accordingly.

Though a shared vision is important, shared outcomes are even more so. Part of the reason transformations fail is because of a lack of accountability. Co-creation of vision and outcome can help your leadership more clearly see their role and accountability within the transformation program.

Finally, to create the change you want to see in your business, your leaders have to embody them as well. They are motivating their teams to do something new, something unknown. A steady hand is important, as is a vision, but role modeling what the behaviors are that produce the outcomes creates a path for others to do the same.

## 3. Get C-Level Buy-In

When you have senior leadership invested in what you're doing to reshape the company, it creates an incredible amount of momentum across their broader teams. Clear sponsorship and support can make all the difference in getting the resources and attention the transformation program will require.

Especially in the early months of the transformation, the success of the first programs is critical. If they fail, it will make it that much harder for programs down the line. The believability in the change itself can start to falter. Senior-level support can drive the right accountability and visibility to sustain the energy around the transformation. As one of our retail clients shared, "The effort you need is high, maybe higher than you need afterwards to get the ball rolling and the execution done. You need commitment across the board and, specifically, commitment to invest and be patient."

## 4. Anchor in Outcomes

In 2015, we worked with a large fast-food company as it transformed how it created convenience for customers. The CEO was keenly aware that the company had not kept pace with the changing customer expectations around it: from the increased expectations on food quality to how to use digital to make the food more accessible. He said, "In the last five years, the world has moved faster outside the business than inside. The business cannot ignore what customers are saying when the message is clear, We're not on our game." We discussed its customer experience and some of the challenges that stood in the way of transforming convenience.

While the need to transform was apparent, the problem he was solving was not just about becoming more digital, or even about improving the customer experience. He was very clear, "Our most important priority remains growing guest counts by serving more customers, more often." The leadership team had developed a solid customer relationship strategy oriented around engaging three customer types and the desired experience for each: Frequents, Regulars, and Occasionals. Yet, in 2016, the company lacked the capability to execute any of it. To do so required a unified view of the customer, customer segmentation, multi-channel capabilities, and marketing automation.

By clearly identifying the business need they were solving for, we were able to partner with this client much more effectively by defining critical metrics and a maturity model, baselining gaps to the target state, and building a plan to close the gaps. This guided the work to connect the right capabilities and test progress against the desired goals. The result was a multi-channel program that produced $200 million in incremental revenue and also started the client on a path to transforming its capabilities through creating a new organization that reduced the time to market of new ideas from 24 months to just three.

Creating clarity on the business outcomes you are solving for is one of the most critical components of a successful transformation. A technology integration program, for instance, is never done purely to upgrade software or even to move to newer platforms, such as the cloud. They are usually initiated to improve efficiency, reduce cost, or improve the customer experience. Without a clear understanding of which of these you are addressing, you can easily fall into the trap of checking off deliverables and outputs, but never getting to the outcomes you desire. This creates the watermelon effect we spoke of in the product chapter: Everything looks green on the outside, but you're red on the inside. It is also why 70% of transformations fail: checking off a service-level agreement (SLA) for a cloud implementation creates a different outcome than testing to see whether you've increased the speed and quality in which the business is delivering on a digital product.

## 5. Seize Your Quick Wins and Communicate

Change is hard. For a lot of people, it raises doubts and insecurities about their ability to traverse the unknown. Running large transformation programs is no different. Quick wins are an important way to signal progress. These wins can cross a number of categories from progress against outcomes, to advancing capabilities, to recognizing progress in the process itself.

As you progress in your transformation journey, it's important that your communications reflect that as well. Though initial communications will likely be more geared toward setting the big strategic picture, your teams will soon want to see operational progress and how their work is contributing to the overall.

People want to see where they fit into the change, but they also want to see how their leaders are reacting to it. It's not just about what you communicate, but how. Authenticity is everything.

## 6. Move Fast

*"This is how we leap frog . . . we need to do more of this!?! How fast can we start working this way?"*

— Large retailer

The benefit every company should be taking advantage of as a result of Moore's Law is that technology can now enable rapid prototyping. In fact, you can go from an idea to a live prototype, using real data, in a matter of weeks. That's pretty exciting.

More and more, we are seeing companies come into "pitch" conversations saying, "Don't tell me what you can do. Show me." Where this is particularly valuable is when you are trying to address underserved or new markets. Rapid prototyping enables you to build out some of your most ambiguous (or ambitious) ideas to see how they translate in real life and what they actually enable.

Take, for instance, a recreational vehicle manufacturer. What started as a prototype of a vehicle configurator quickly turned into a conversation on data and how that data informed the organization. When the clients got it, they realized, "This isn't about a configurator. This is about a translation layer that underpins our entire org, which, yes, could enable a configurator, but has a myriad of other uses." Bingo!

Where prototypes bring ideas rapidly to life, pilots are key to testing and learning. One of our energy clients was seeing a huge strain on the energy grid as a result of growing energy consumption. They wanted to find a way to reduce the strain on the power grid by applying digital to get customers to use less energy. This is where the integration of capabilities becomes critical because the outcomes they were driving were to reduce energy consumption by driving behavior change. Using strategy, experience, data, and engineering, an app was piloted with 2,000 customers that enabled them to visualize their habits, identify actionable insights, compare their usage with their own history as well as with the consumption of their neighbors, and earn badges for a job well done.

Though the client had launched time-of-use pricing, which charges lower rates during off-peak hours as an incentive for customers to spread out their energy usage, the app coupled that with behavioral data and applied gamification to get people to start being more conscious of their usage. For the energy company, it provided a way to test how to activate various pricing options before finally landing on what made most sense for the business.

Whatever your entry point into transformation, the most important thing is that you have a clear vision of the outcomes you're trying to drive and that you start to chart the path to get there. How you get there will continue to evolve over time, but taking those first steps and embracing the change are what will get you to the future.

## 7. Be Thoughtful About Your Governance Choices

At the end of the day, everything presented in this book comes down to the team that's executing it. This team will own holding the frame on the impact you want to create for customers, how that creates value for your business, the technological and operational implications of those decisions, and whether your execution is achieving the intended outcomes. This team could include cross-functional leadership from within your company as well as your partners.

In a lot of ways, setting out to transform your business is like building a start-up. The team needs to include people who balance critical expertise with a belief in the vision you are creating together. That latter point cannot be reiterated enough. Leading through change is not easy and doing so with a team that is not aligned on the outcomes is near impossible.

So, what should you look for when designing the team?

- Leaders who are signed up to the vision of where the company needs to go
- Members who have meaningful role in the organization and/or control of sizable business unit that will lead the way for the broader organization
- The core team has to be cross-functional and multi-disciplinary
- Any external partners should be there because they fill a specific gap on the team – this could be capability-specific or they could be there because of their strength in governance

This transformation team should sign off on the key projects happening in the organization and be empowered to make the call on whether those projects support the transformation or not.

Deciding what level of leadership is part of the team is also an important consideration. A few years ago, I was working with a leader at a bank who was making a call as to who would lead a key transformation program in their mortgages division. The head of the mortgages group suggested one of his direct reports. We see this all the time. The reality of stretched schedules lends itself to delegating to someone who can dedicate the time required, but it also presents a challenge. If the leader of the mortgages division was not aligned to the transformation initiative and the change involved, they could very easily revert to protecting the status quo. Things could very easily go off the rails because now the transformation lead would be going against their direct supervisor to execute on the vision of the transformation. On the flip side, if the mortgages lead is in charge, then their number two will step up because they know their boss will have much better perspective on the change required and the transformation ahead.

## 8. Choose Partners Who Will Co-create and Are a Fit for Your Team

One thing about the idea of partner ecosystems is it's no longer just about a partner to whom you can outsource capability. Today's partner ecosystems are composed of partners who fill your capability gaps and also play a critical role in co-creation.

This ecosystem will likely have partners who play different roles within your transformation and, as a result, the criteria may look different for each. Your transformation partner may need to bridge vision, business perspective, and technological expertise. For instance, if your transformation partner is focused on cost reduction in isolation, they will be unlikely to help your organization reach its full potential. Meanwhile, your change management partner may anchor more strongly on structure, process, behaviors, reporting, and communications.

As much as the tangible characteristics of your partners are important, so are the intangibles. Do your partners engender trust? Are they the kind of people you want to work with on a day-to-day basis? How will they collaborate to bring your teams on the journey? With partners, the how is just as important as the what.

## 9. Keep Your Teams Small and Cross-functional

Today's teams need to think and act quickly. As we mentioned earlier, one component of this moving with speed and agility is smaller, autonomous teams. One of the biggest challenges within any established organization is breaking through operational silos that limit innovation. Small, multidisciplinary teams provide a way to break through those silos and create progress faster.

For one of our large banking clients, we broke down its 1,500-person engineering team into more manageable clusters of 200 people. For each cohort of 200, we put in place a core of agile coaches, engineers, operations people, creative designers, strategists, business analysts, and other champions. They liaised across the different service lines, acting as a kind of guild of technical professionals, i.e., the modern world's master craftspeople. The approach changed the way the company approached its engineering function and enabled them to bring the desired products to market much faster.

You can also see the power of smaller teams in prototyping and piloting efforts. Rapid response teams, for instance, bring together a small, diverse set of capability leaders to bring prototypes to life in a matter of weeks.

# 10. Consider New Approaches to Funding That Match the Way Projects Work

One of the operational hurdles many of our clients face is that their businesses are not wired to fund an environment of continuous improvement. Most financial systems are still structured around the ideas of time, cost, and scope where funding is linked to a business case with a specific return on investment (ROI). This is inconsistent with a continuous life cycle where products are constantly evolving.

In addition, budget cycles are managed yearly or quarterly at best. Now think about the life cycle of value creation laid out through the PS How or the principles of Agile shared in the product chapter. The reality is that, as your company becomes more sophisticated in its digital capability, the faster it will need to move. Programs certainly can't wait for annual budget cycles and likely will need to move more quickly than quarterly as well.

One of the options mentioned earlier was a VC-funding approach where teams pitch ideas on a more frequent basis to gain funding for phases of work. This is similar to the Series A, B, and C funding mechanism for start-ups. Instead of funding the end outcome upfront, funding is based on meeting specific milestones.

Another approach is to look at your transformation as from a portfolio perspective. This aligns to the portfolio approach to defend, differentiate, and disrupt from the strategy chapter. Instead of making one big bet, make a series of bets across your business. This can help de-risk your overall portfolio while creating space for innovation.

Taken together, this list can help you get ahead of some of the most common pitfalls in digital business transformation programs and build a solid foundation to execute from.

# CHAPTER 13

# What Transformation Journeys Actually Look Like

## They Are Never a Straight Line

Like the people who are part of them, no two companies are the same. Over my 25 years consulting to some of the world's most well-known brands, every company comes with its own culture, operations, assets, vision, and internal relationship dynamics. As a result, they also enter their transformation journeys differently.

There are many who aren't even thinking about "transformation"; rather, they are just constantly evolving their business and through that process are transforming. For others, they have intentionally taken on transformation as a goal. Some take on sizable transformation programs aimed at changing the way they work. Others decide to focus on transforming a specific capability incrementally. Still others will enter through new products. Many will pilot, test, learn, and scale. Along the way there will be lessons, adjustments, and redirections. This journey is never a straight line.

In 2017, we were in conversations with the leadership of a global hospitality company. The CEO outlined what it was seeing in the market: The hospitality model was being disrupted by the likes of Airbnb, it saw the possibilities of expanding its services outside of hotel clients and to the broader communities around them, and it believed there was an opportunity to create a trusted platform for independent hotel chains, including ones that were not in the current network of hotels. The idea was very compelling in that it was setting out to be a new breed of hotel company whose customers included not only hotel occupants but local residents.

At the time, it had also made the choice to take on a series of acquisitions and partnerships. These would not only expand the footprint to different types of hotels but would advance the kinds of services it could bring to their customers.

Everything it was doing was very compelling business strategy. We worked together to envision how these choices would translate to a world that is digital. The idea was to create a connected platform that utilized existing capabilities while addressing gaps that had been identified through the process.

Similar to what's been shared in previous chapters, the execution would rest on the ability to bring capabilities together while working in new ways that allowed for continuous improvement. The unique aspect of this company's transformation journey was not just the outcomes it was trying to drive, but the fact that it was doing so in the midst of acquiring a number of different companies. This is where these choices get complex. When studies show that 70–90% of acquisitions fail, how do you then think about integrating multiple new companies while fundamentally evolving the way you work? The company decided they wanted to proceed with its own team, took the thinking forward, and adapted the work to the idea.

In early 2020, we reconnected with the CEO and leadership team. They told us about the steps they had taken since those conversations in 2017. They had progressed the transformation but decided to do so through a series of distinct IT and customer programs. Though this advanced some of the offerings, the company came to a similar conclusion many clients do: its siloed approach wasn't producing the outcomes they wanted to drive. It wasn't able to build the connected platform it set out to create. Because the efforts weren't connected, the company would now need to redesign the next iteration by reworking what it did in silos to create the new ways of working that were critical to those outcomes.

Though the leadership team was energized to hit reset and push for creating a truly disruptive and transformational platform, the reality was a number of steps that had to happen first in order to do so, from resetting its cost base to focusing on a couple of strategic programs that would make the most impact on moving the platform idea forward. It couldn't do everything it had originally planned, but now has a path to address the foundational areas that were holding it back, while taking thoughtful steps forward.

The reality is that most companies are not brand new to digital business transformation. There are a multitude of factors and decisions along the way, some incredibly powerful and truly transformative and others disconnected missteps. What's important is doing exactly what our client did: always taking an honest look at whether the choices you're making are driving the outcomes you seek and, if they are not, making the brave choice to redirect and get on a better path.

## They Require Treating Digital as More Than a Channel

Digital business transformation is not just about your capabilities; it's about rewiring how you create value. Every company has fundamental beliefs about how they provide value. For established businesses these beliefs can be so strongly held that they feel like unwritten law: They are the foundations from which the business was built, around which many of its people spent their careers creating successful products, services, capabilities, and processes, and culturally these beliefs produce a sense of pride and community that feels existential in and of itself.

When leaders step foot on the path to digitally transforming their companies, they are not just providing the same value in different channels, but are changing how their company (and the people within it) creates value. This is a mental shift that has implications for the allocation of capital. If you believe you are a car manufacturer, you will invest in manufacturing and dealerships, but will you invest in mobility? Maybe not. This is the *inversion* dynamic discussed in the Gryphon chapter: recognizing that the new ideas you adopt will likely conflict with your existing industry and business.[1]

Below is a list of digital entrants who have created Direct-to-Consumer (DTC) businesses with massive valuations:

- Warby Parker, valued at $1.75 billion
- Dollar Shave Club, acquired by Unilever for $1 billion
- Casper and Harry's, each valued at about $750 million apiece
- Glossier, valued at $390 million
- Bonobos, acquired for $310 million
- BarkBox, worth between $150 and $200 million

For established consumer packaged goods (CPG) companies, their business model is anchored in being a supplier of products to retailers. Analysis from eMarketer/Publicis Sapient projects that DTC for CPG companies will grow to about 15% market penetration by 2024, up from 11% reported in 2020. More aggressive growth cases forecast market penetration of up to 20% by 2024, almost double the amount of customer reach CPGs are experiencing today.[2]

Now take a moment and ask yourself how well Luxottica, one of the world's largest eyeglass manufacturers, could compete with Warby Parker by adding ecommerce functionality to its website. It would be providing the same value it always has (popular eyewear) through a different channel (ecommerce). You can quickly see that while on the surface this seems like a straightforward, apples-to-apples comparison, it really isn't.

In 2014, famed venture capitalist Mary Meeker described what she called the "Internet trifecta" known as the 3 Cs: content, community, and commerce. These are a few of the components that come together to create strong digital commerce offerings. What Warby Parker created is not just a channel to sell similar products but solid products combined with an experience and business model that meet the needs of customers. That is what established companies are competing with: entirely different digital-based business models.

Hopefully, if you've come this far in this book, you can see that what it takes to create great digital products, services, and experiences is much more than the capability to do what you've always done, but just in a different channel. Digital business transformation is just that, transforming your business to be digital so you, in turn, can have the capability to be competitive in a digital world.

# They Are Almost Always Driven by Uncertainty

The level of uncertainty businesses face in the context of digital is driven by two things: whether someone understands your customers' needs better than you do and whether they can apply digital to disrupt how those needs are met. The greater the uncertainty, the more profound the need for transformation.

In 2017, we were in conversations with the chairman of one of the world's largest retailers. He began the meeting with only one agenda item, "What to do about Amazon and the growth of the Amazon Prime service?" Though Amazon competed on price and selection, brick-and-mortar retailers always had the convenience factor of being able to provide products in-store the same day. Now Amazon was creating a direct threat to this key component of differentiation.

When COVID-19 hit in early 2020, this dynamic was magnified. Retailers in the grocery and essential goods space saw a massive shift to online that they were not prepared for. In the United States, in-store grocery revenue jumped up 150%, while online skyrocketed up 700%. This created a surge in revenue, but it wasn't always profitable due to how supply chains were structured. To keep up with that demand retailers hired more workers, which continued to exacerbate profitability challenges.

If you are a retailer and Amazon is your greatest threat, you have by default been thrown into a highly uncertain context. Not only do you have to account for Amazon's impact on customer expectations of retail, but as it proliferates its own products, such as the Amazon Basics line, it directly impacts the demand for your inventory.

From our client's perspective, the challenge it was facing with Amazon Prime was not just one of supply chain and distribution, it was about customer experience. The company's long history with its customers had built a high degree of trust in the company and the quality of the goods compared with the diversity of Amazon suppliers. But it also knew that there was a higher level of customer experience expectations that hadn't been fully addressed. This uncertainty and disruption was triggering the need to not only assess its own capabilities, but determine what it could realistically deliver that would be differentiated for its customers.

When you think about this example, there is probably no more menacing digital competitor than Amazon. By 2017, it had $177 billion in revenues, with an average growth rate of 28% for the prior decade. Yet, most digital disruptors don't set out to upturn an industry. They start by seeing a customer need and creating a completely new way to address it. In his book *Unlocking the Customer Value Chain,* Thales S. Teixeira examined this dynamic and concluded that digital disruptors didn't enter markets to steal share; they focus on stealing a select few customer activities.[3] Figure 13.1 illustrates our own assessment of which disruptors are impacting incumbents by identifying and addressing specific changing customer needs.

Looking at the disruptors on this list you can see they range from mid-size companies to digital behemoths. This is why having a plan around where you want to play on the digital spectrum is important. Whether you are already being disrupted or if your industry's disruption has been relatively minimal, having the capability to see and address customer pain points rapidly and effectively is critical to how you will compete.

| Industry | Incumbent | Disruptor |
|---|---|---|
| Financial services | Wells Fargo | Venmo |
| Energy | Exxon Mobil | Grid+ |
| Pharmaceuticals | Pfizer | TrueTag |
| Hospitality | Hilton | Airbnb |
| Retail | Target | Amazon |
| Automotive | Ford | Lyft |
| Insurance | State Farm | Inshure |
| Luxury | Gucci | Vegea |
| Pharmacy | CVS | TruePill |
| Telecom | AT&T | WhatsApp |
| Consumer Products | Reckitt Benckiser | Loop |
| Travel | American Airlines | Priceline |

**FIGURE 13.1** Changing customer needs drive industry disruption

## Without a Clear Vision, Functions Get Disconnected Fast

When was the first time you heard about AI? If you were born after the millennium, it may have always existed in some aspect of your day-to-day life. If you grew up in the second half of the twentieth century, your first memories were probably from colorful depictions in science fiction films like *2001: A Space Odyssey*, *Star Wars*, *Blade Runner, The Terminator,* and the list goes on and on.

In 1970, famed cognitive scientist and AI leader Marvin Minsky told *Life* magazine, "from three to eight years we will have a machine with the general intelligence of an average human being." The idea of AI feels so contemporary, like it was birthed in Silicon Valley, but in the 1970s, Minsky and others had created the principles of machine learning and powerful algorithms that proved how AI could work. But, as we know, a human level of AI would not surface in the 1970s, not because the understanding wasn't there but because there wasn't the computational power and storage needed to bring it to life.[4]

This is a similar dynamic that companies run into with their digital business transformations. One of the most consistent challenges we see is companies that invest in one capability area, advance it significantly, but soon realize they can't create their desired outcomes until they get the other capability areas to progress in sync. What often happens is leadership in one part of the business will take on a transformation program specific to their functional area. So, you may have an incredibly sophisticated engineering capability but cannot create more sophisticated products because the experience function isn't capable of fully leveraging it, and vice versa. This is why having a connected view of your digital business transformation efforts is important and why they are ideally led by the C-suite who can have a view across the entirety.

Just as with the evolution of AI, you can have the vision, but until the pieces come together, you will be limited by your least-developed capability. When the divergence becomes too great, you basically have to stop and start your transformation again in order to solve both the capability issue and to create the ways of working across capabilities. With a destination in mind, you can check to see if your incremental efforts are moving you in the right direction. Without a destination in mind, you are almost guaranteed to create transformation debt you'll have to reconcile later.

## The Many Paths to Transformation

Once you've identified the outcomes you're trying to drive and where you want to play in the spectrum of digital, how do you begin to unlock value? Let's go back to the beginning for a moment. To digitally transform your business requires transforming not only what your customers see, buy, and experience, but how your enterprise operates to enable that. Figure 13.2 shows a model we refer to as the "Nine Box." It covers the high-level buckets that any digital business transformation could touch on.

The "Value Exchange" thread highlights the key interaction points between the company and the customer. Companies must consider new data-driven products and services, innovative experiences and ecosystems, and the overall communications points with consumers.

**FIGURE 13.2** "Nine Box" of digital business transformation

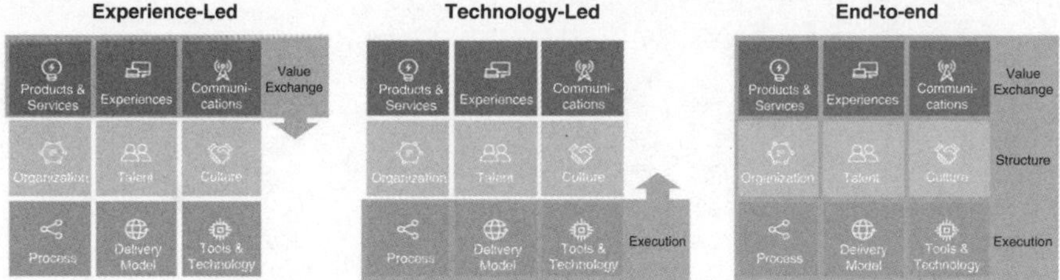


**FIGURE 13.3** Entry points to digital business transformation

The "Structure" thread addresses how the organization is set up to perform daily operations. It includes how teams are organized, the talent and skillsets of the employees, and the overall culture of the workplace along with the incentive system driving behavior.

The "Execution" thread addresses how companies operate to deliver their products and services. It includes the process and methodologies the organization leverages, the delivery model for bringing about both step change and daily tasks, and the underlying technology to enable business operations.

Companies choose a number of paths to enter their transformations, as seen in Figure 13.3.

In the summer of 2020, we were speaking to the Chief Digital Officer (CDO) of a large auto manufacturer. She wanted to know three things: How is consumer behavior evolving? How is technology evolving? What are the implications for our industry? We got into a winding conversation covering everything from consumer expectations of a frictionless experience, to fewer people driving, to the idea of cars as platforms. It was an end-to-end conversation covering both the consumer and enterprise areas of transformation.

For a large French grocer, the challenge was in connecting the digital assets across organizational silos and creating the capability in-house to manage through change. Though this certainly had implications for value exchange, it was grounded in transforming the enterprise through improving both structure and execution.

Truth be told, there is no right way to enter into transformation. Most often it's driven by the most pressing need in the business. And that's OK. Where companies falter is when they take a myopic view of transformation through a single function or capability. Through the lessons in this book, you now have a frame to see implications beyond those immediate choices and start to carve out a path that will move you toward not just improving a function but creating value in a completely different way.

# CHAPTER 14

# The Beginning

*"Now this is not the end. It is not even the beginning of the end. But it is, perhaps, the end of the beginning."*

— Winston Churchill

## Why There Is No "End"

As you approach the close of this book, it is – and without wishing to make light of Winston Churchill's famous 1942 quote or the circumstances leading up to it – not the end or even the beginning of the end, but it may represent a new beginning.

In truth, it is likely that the reader of this book is already somewhere along their transformation journey. Perhaps you have taken on a widescale transformation program that is currently permeating through your organization and is impacting the way that you work. Maybe you have applied a transformational approach to one customer journey, a specific capability, or digitized a product or service and are looking to move on to the next stage. Those programs may have left you frustrated; they didn't achieve the outcomes you expected because the efforts weren't connected across the organization. Just as likely, the programs or sizable transformations were successful but the world moved on. As we've learned, change is constant and accelerating.

Digital business transformation is a journey that trumps its destination: a journey that asks businesses to reimagine and rapidly realize new ways of working and satisfying consumer expectations. It is the process of helping your organization reinvent itself against the backdrop of unprecedented data, technology, and, ultimately, consumer-driven change which is fueling unexpected competitive dynamics and diminishing traditional business models as industries shift and merge.

One of the key things that differentiates digital business transformation from conventional digital transformation is that it sits at the confluence of changing human behavior and the reality that leading businesses, across every industry, are now built on technology and software. Constant evolution and the capability to deliver it require more of business leaders than simply regarding change as a project with a starting point and a completion.

In reality, it poses a different meaning for each organization and utilizes different tools to answer the unique questions of each business, every time. Your digital business transformation is, or will be, circular and not a straight line. Done right, the world outside won't be able to see where the "digital" part of your business begins, where it ends, or how to breach the digital moat you've created.

## Where Do We Go from Here?

Here's a question: do you believe the change in front of us is greater than the change behind? It's not a question that many of us take the time to consider. The answer should be easy: "yes." It is, after all, little more than 300 years since Thomas Newcomen's "atmospheric steam engine" ushered in the industrial revolution. As Kurzweil's Law of Accelerating Returns shows us, the rate of technical progress doubles roughly every decade, which means we will witness 1,000 times more technological progress in the twenty-first century than we did in the twentieth century.

All evidence suggests, though, that most of us are not constantly future-gazing and then planning for that future. Instead, we are reacting to what has just happened or to something that is on our immediate horizon. And, do you know what? That's absolutely fine. No one is suggesting that you need to be a soothsayer, able to strategize for an unknown future and harness technologies not yet invented. Sometimes, being able to react to a situational change – even one that is far from desirable – is what brings about your competitive advantage. To take action at the "defend" end of the defend-differentiate-disrupt spectrum can be just what is required to set your organization on the path to a brighter digital future. If, that is, you meet the challenge with positivity, creativity, agility, and, most important of all, with an explicit understanding that your immediate and successful solution to the challenge at hand was just the end of the beginning. You've topped up your digital moat and now you're not going to let it stagnate or dry up, are you?

It is said that necessity is the mother of invention. For all of the commercial challenges caused by the COVID-19 pandemic, it also acted as a launchpad for established companies as well as start-ups to take a fresh look at a changed world and reorient themselves to provide the products and services that create customer and business value, and keep them relevant in a digital age. Let me give you an example of how that can work.

One of the sectors that has outperformed most others since the outbreak of the pandemic is online grocery, with sales in some markets nearly doubling during lockdown.[1] Conversely, efforts to reduce single-use plastics have stalled, in part due to the increase in use of face masks, gloves, and disposable wipes and partly because general recycling rates have plummeted during lockdown. Into this scenario steps Loop, the online shopping service already established in the United States and France, and now riding the wave with expansion into the United Kingdom, Japan, Australia, Canada, and Germany. What sets Loop apart is that it aims to eliminate plastic waste by delivering food, drink, and household items in reusable packaging. Backed by major consumer goods companies, such as Unilever and PepsiCo and by a major supermarket retailer in each of those markets, customers receive their orders in refillable containers that can be cleaned and reused up to 100 times.

Loop is a success story made possible, or at least accelerated by, a confluence of factors coming out of the pandemic: a massive increase in and unfulfilled demand for online grocery delivery; a permanent shift in consumer behaviors as a proportion of the customers who adopted online delivery during lockdown continue to use the service; an unmet need both of customers and manufacturers to reduce and recycle plastic waste; and, underpinning it all, the adoption of technology by businesses and consumers, to replace what was previously an in-store experience.

Wherever you looked, among the negative news stories necessarily coming out of the pandemic, there were bright spots. In the automotive industry, the long-term downward trend in individual car ownership, particularly among younger city dwellers, began to reverse. In China, one of the first countries to come out of lockdown, car sales were peaking higher in 2020 than the previous year and indications are that the trend will be repeated in the United States and Europe as people avoid public transport and put safety first. In a similar, eco-friendly vein, governments everywhere are reprioritizing transport policies to try to capture some of the environmental benefits that were witnessed during their respective lockdown periods. New cycle-friendly initiatives are being rolled out in cities worldwide, amid a global boom in bicycle sales. Regulation to allow personal mobility solutions, such as rental e-scooters, has been fast-tracked – freeing the way for digital companies such as Bird, Scoot, Lime, and Jump to enter new markets with their nascent operating models.

Everywhere, established companies are reporting significant increases in revenue from ecommerce. L'Oréal, for instance, has seen significant growth in ecommerce even in its less developed markets – reporting an online sales jump of 300% in Latin America in April 2020 and 400% in Africa and the Middle East. In the first quarter of 2020, it saw ecommerce sales across the group grow by 53% compared with a year earlier. L'Oréal's chief digital officer, Lubomira Rochet, said, "The crisis has profoundly accelerated the digital transformation of the beauty sector. In ecommerce, we achieved in eight weeks what it would have otherwise taken us three years to do." Crucially, the company believes many consumer behaviors, including the use of virtual try-ons for make-up and hair color and one-on-one beauty consultations via video chat, will last after the pandemic subsides.[2]

Do you think that those companies and industries, and many others beside them, will take their foot off the gas now that they have survived and successfully navigated through the coronavirus crisis? It's unlikely. For all that understanding and accepting that digital business transformation is a journey, a perennial project requiring constant attention and hard work, the taste of successes along the way can be addictive.

Remember that image of Mo Farah crossing the finish line to take the gold medal and the expression on his face changing from one of pain to elation, even then knowing he'd have to go out and do it all over again if he wanted to stay champion? If you've reached this far in the book, then I hope and assume that you are your own Mo Farah, ready to do the hard miles but most definitely up for the victories along the way.

## What's in Your Digital Moat?

Knowing that every company and organization is different, and that the content and different types of digital moat will be as myriad as your industry sectors and market circumstances, *Digital Business Transformation* is written as a guide to help you do just that: to begin and keep building your moat and to fuel your competitiveness in a digital world.

What you build and the way you build it will be different from what the next reader builds, which is why I haven't provided you with a blueprint. I have, though, equipped you with the necessary building materials, the components of capability and organization to aid you in its construction.

## What Are You Building?

Digital business transformation is, at its core, about changing the way you think and operate as an organization. While technology is implicit in your digital moat, it is not the technology itself that provides you with competitive advantage. Your digital moat is the sum of the capabilities you put in place to navigate change, create value, and be competitive in a digital world.

The technology is crucial though. It is, and will continue to be, the most tangible of the forces of connected change, disrupting every company, in every industry, in every market through its impact on our lives and the lives of our customers. Technology will ultimately determine which players survive and prosper and which diminish and fail.

This book highlights the opportunity, as well as the threat, that fundamental and accelerating technological evolution represents. To be great at reimagining the future of your business will first require identifying and eliminating those powerful brakes and blocks within an organization that may well define your success today but will hinder efforts to transform as a leading business for tomorrow. That transformation means thinking differently about every one of the capabilities that will drive future business outcomes: strategy, product, experience, engineering, data, and the attributes of organizational change necessary to become a Gryphon organization.

In a digital age, for your organization to thrive will require that these capability areas work in concert with the right organizational characteristics: to create a model that gives your organization the ability to more effectively navigate changes in customer, business, and market demands.

I hope that the guidance, examples, case studies, and frameworks that I have shared in *Digital Business Transformation* will help your organization to flourish and drive business outcomes through its ability to evolve products, services, and experiences that continually align with changing customer behaviors and technology.

## Everyday Superheroes

As a small child, I had limited fine motor skills. A lack of strength and dexterity in my hand meant that writing and creating was a real challenge. Although I couldn't write well, discovering computers helped me to type, create, and much more. Ever since, I've been passionate about the way that technology can be implemented and improved to enhance people's and organizations' capabilities.

It's no coincidence that the Marvel heroes who inspired me back then – Captain America, the Hulk, Spiderman, Iron Man – always had a little engineered help among their suite of superpowers. That sowed a seed with me. Technology has the transformative ability to imagine new futures and improve people's lives.

Later, as a young man, I had the privilege of meeting Nelson Mandela. I had co-founded a company that delivered Internet, consulting, and connectivity solutions. Among our achievements was to leverage advances in vertical blanking interval (VBI) technology to encrypt data and broadcast to remote areas that lacked connectivity, sub-Saharan Africa for one where local schools benefited from a curriculum broadcast to them digitally. It had not been so many years since he had been released from prison, and Mandela was his nation's hero and a global leader. Nonetheless, he took the time to encourage me in those early endeavors and to recognize, as I still do, that technology has the transformative ability to make a difference in the world and to people's lives.

I don't have the same Marvel heroes anymore, but individuals such as Mandela have become heroes and I do have historic and contemporary figures who inspire me and cause me to wonder, some of whom appear in this book. If there is something that unites them, and which is at the root of my admiration for them, it is that they all rejected the idea that there is a set way in which things work, that cannot be reimagined and remolded. It's this outlook that drives me and I hope you to challenge and change convention, by harnessing emerging technology to transform businesses and make a difference.

My life experience is different from your experience, which is different from the experience of others. That said, I'm prepared to take a bet that whatever your role is, whatever your company does, and whatever industry you operate in, we all have certain motivations in common: to build, to make better, to realize the future, and in some manner to change the world around us.

Books are read by individuals. Digital business transformation is brought about by teams. Success belongs to groups and is rarely the result of individual endeavor. Real, enduring change is never the legacy of a single person; however, much history books might try to tell us otherwise. In *Digital Business Transformation*, I have used the terms "you" and "your" a lot. In truth, in the 30 years Publicis Sapient has been in business and in my 25 years meeting and helping established organizations on the transformation of their business, the greatest achievements I've witnessed have come about as a result of exceptional teamwork.

You, the reader, may be the leader, bringing people along the journey with you into the future, or you may be a core part of that team. Whichever it is, your success at transforming your organization will depend on a shared understanding of what you want to be in the world, a collective commitment to change, and a unity of spirit, endeavor, and effort.

I'd like to share with you one of my favorite quotes, from the cultural anthropologist Margaret Mead. It's not only a favorite, it is also, as I'm sure my colleagues will attest, the one that I use most often, sometimes to inspire them, but as often to recognize their extraordinary achievements. I share it with you now in the hope that your team – current or future – can achieve the transformative change and success you are looking for:

> *"Never doubt that a small group of thoughtful, committed citizens can change the world; indeed, it's the only thing that ever has."*

Throughout *Digital Business Transformation*, I have stressed the importance of identifying and unlocking value for the customer and for your business. Implicit in this is financial success and reward. I don't tell you what that "value" is, for that will be different for every organization dependent on their circumstance. I can tell you what it looks like though.

For every digitally native entrant, for every established business, for every client of Publicis Sapient, value is realized when you enable human potential. Your digital moat, your SPEED capabilities of strategy, product, experience, engineering, and data, as well as the change culture you elicit for your organization – all these are lined up in service of making a difference. When we create a digital product or service that makes people's lives easier, when we make an experience even more frictionless, when we use digital to enable people to do something they couldn't do before or do it better or more quickly, when we give them the sense of having acquired an everyday superpower; that is what I mean by improving people's lives. That is what "value" looks like. That, ultimately, is what *Digital Business Transformation* is all about.

# Notes

## Preface


1. Warren Buffett, Berkshire Hathaway 1995 Annual Meeting, Warren Buffett Archive, CNBC, May 1, 1995, https://buffett.cnbc.com/video/1995/05/01/buffett-most-moats-arent-worth-a-damn.html, accessed September 3, 2020.
2. Satya Nadella, regarding Microsoft Q3 earnings call, "Microsoft Saw Two Years of Digital Transformation Happen in Two Months," Business Standard website, April 29, 2020, https://www.business-standard.com/article/international/microsoft-sees-yearlong-digital-transformation-happen-in-2-months-nadella-120043000184_1.html, accessed September 8, 2020.


## Chapter 1: The Death of Business as Usual


1. Landmarks Preservation Commission, Number 3 LP-0889, July 22, 1975, http://s-media.nyc.gov/agencies/lpc/lp/0889.pdf, accessed September 9, 2020.
2. Erin Wayman, "Becoming Human: The Evolution of Walking Upright," *Smithsonian Magazine,* August 6, 2012, https://www.smithsonianmag.com/science-nature/becoming-human-the-evolution-of-walking-upright-13837658/, accessed September 9, 2020.
3. Ray Kurzweil, "The Law of Accelerating Returns," The Kurzweil Library, March 7, 2001, https://www.kurzweilai.net/the-law-of-accelerating-returns, accessed September 9, 2020.
4. Jake Siegel, "Cameron Says Microsoft's Role in Avatar Was Key," Microsoft Services, February 5, 2010, https://web.archive.org/web/20120106163618/http://www.microsoft.com/microsoftservices/en/us/article_Microsoft_Role_In_Avatar.aspx, accessed September 9, 2020.
5. UCLA Anderson, "Leaders on Leadership: Robert A. Iger, The Walt Disney Company," YouTube, August 8, 2016, https://www.youtube.com/watch?v=0J1K61bYP5A, accessed September 9, 2020.
6. "The Walt Disney Company Announces Strategic Reorganization," Walt Disney Company website, March 14, 2018, https://thewaltdisneycompany.com/walt-disney-company-announces-strategic-reorganization/, accessed September 9, 2020.

7. Wharton School, University of Pennsylvania, "Bob Iger: Why Disney Is Betting Big on Streaming," November 12, 2019, Knowledge@Wharton, https://knowledge.wharton.upenn.edu/article/bog-iger-disney-betting-big-streaming/, accessed September 9, 2020.
8. Jessica Bursztynsky, "Disney Says It Now Has 54.5 Million Disney+ Subscribers," CNBC (May 5, 2020), https://www.cnbc.com/2020/05/05/disney-reports-33point5-million-disney-plus-subscribers-at-end-of-q2.html, accessed September 9, 2020.

# Chapter 2: The Four Forces of Connected Change

1. Henry Ford, *My Life and Work* (New York: Doubleday, 1922), 72.
2. Sohaib Athar, Twitter post, May 2, 2011, https://twitter.com/ReallyVirtual/status/64780730286358528.
3. "The LEGO Brand," LEGO website, https://www.lego.com/en-us/aboutus/lego-group/the-lego-brand, accessed September 9, 2020.
4. "Tomorrow's Capitalism Inquiry," Volans website, https://volans.com/project/tomorrows-capitalism-inquiry/, accessed September 9, 2020.

# Chapter 3: What Is Slowing Down Established Businesses? – Blocks, Brakes and Behaviors

1. Till Alexander Leopold, Vesselina Stefanova Ratcheva, and Saadia Zahidi, "The Future of Jobs Report 2018," World Economic Forum website, September 17, 2018, pp. 8, 13, https://www.weforum.org/reports/the-future-of-jobs-report-2018, accessed September 9, 2020.
2. Yannick Binvel, Michael Franzino, Alan Guarino, Jean-Marc Laouchez, Werner Penk, "The Global Talent Crunch," Korn Ferry website, Spring 2018, p. 16, https://www.kornferry.com/content/dam/kornferry/docs/article-migration/FOWTalentCrunchFinal_Spring2018.pdf, accessed September 9, 2020.
3. Gerald C. Kane, Doug Palmer, Anh Nguyen Phillips, David Kiron, Natasha Buckley, "Aligning the Organization for Its Digital Future,"

*MIT Sloan Management Review* and Deloitte University Press, July 26, 2016, http://www.enterprisesolutions.tsg.com/sites/default/files/Deloitte%20-%20Aligning%20the%20Organization%20for%20Its%20Digital%20Future.pdf, accessed September 9, 2020.

4. Heather Boushey and Sarah Jane Glynn, "There Are Significant Business Costs to Replacing Employees," Center for American Progress website, November 16, 2012, https://www.americanprogress.org/wp-content/uploads/2012/11/CostofTurnover.pdf, accessed September 9, 2020.

## Chapter 5: The Big Hairy Audacious Goals (BHAGs) of Digital Business Transformation

1. George Stalk, Jr., and Thomas M. Hout, *Competing Against Time: How Time-Based Competition Is Reshaping Global Markets* (New York: The Free Press/Simon & Schuster, 1990).

## Chapter 6: Strategy

1. Guy Theraulaz and Eric Bonabeau, "A Brief History of Stigmergy," *Artificial Life* vol. 5, no. 20 (February 1, 1999), pp. 97–116, https://www.researchgate.net/publication/12680033_A_Brief_History_of_Stigmergy, accessed September 9, 2020.
2. Regarding customer reviews functionality on the original Amazon website, Version Museum website, https://www.versionmuseum.com/history-of/amazon-website, accessed September 9, 2020; Jared Spool, "The Question That Makes Amazon $2.7 Billion of Revenue," Business Insider website, March 28 2009, https://www.businessinsider.com/the-magic-behind-amazons-27-billion-dollar-question-2009-3, accessed September 9, 2020.
3. Jeffrey M. O'Brien, "Business Paradigm Shifts and Free Tequila Shots," *Fortune* (July 10, 2007), https://archive.fortune.com/magazines/fortune/fortune_archive/2007/07/23/100134489/index.htm, accessed September 9, 2020.
4. Sarah Kessler, "Nest: The Story Behind the World's Most Beautiful Thermostat," Mashable website, December 15, 2011, https://mashable.com/2011/12/15/nest-labs-interview/, accessed September 9, 2020.

5. "Most Banks Will Be Made Irrelevant by 2030 – Gartner," Finextra website, October 29, 2018 https://www.finextra.com/newsarticle/32860/most-banks-will-be-made-irrelevant-by-2030---gartner?_lrsc=031222e2-9a9b-457c-8a45-755ce6af121a, accessed September 9, 2020.

# Chapter 7: Product

1. Neil McElroy's 800-Word Memo, Marketing Brand Teams, May13, 1931, https://3lsqjy1sj7i027fcn749gutj-wpengine.netdna-ssl.com/wp-content/uploads/2015/10/McElroyBrandMan.pdf, accessed September 9, 2020; Nirmalya Kumar, "Kill a Brand, Keep a Customer," *Harvard Business Review,* December 2003. https://hbr.org/2003/12/kill-a-brand-keep-a-customer, accessed September 9, 2020.
2. "The HP Way," Hewlett-Packard website, 1980, p. 8, https://www.hpalumni.org/HPWayBooklet1980.pdf, accessed September 9, 2020.
3. "The Toyota Way – Continuous Improvement and Respect for People in Everything We Do," Toyota website, https://www.toyota-europe.com/world-of-toyota/this-is-toyota/the-toyota-way, accessed September 9, 2020.
4. Martin Cagan, *Inspired: How to Create Tech Products Customers Love*, 2nd ed., Chapter 6 (Hoboken, NJ: Wiley, 2018) (originally published 2008).
5. Blake Morgan, "Companies That Failed at Digital Transformation and What We Can Learn from Them," *Forbes* CMO newsletter, Forbes website, September 30, 2019, https://www.forbes.com/sites/blakemorgan/2019/09/30/companies-that-failed-at-digital-transformation-and-what-we-can-learn-from-them/#1e44f190603c, accessed September 9, 2020.
6. Martin Cagan, *Inspired,* Chapter 7.
7. Barbara Chai, "How Publicis Sapient Is Dataful in the Way We Work," Publicis Sapient website, https://www.publicissapient.com/insights/publicis_sapient_is_dataful_in_how_we_work, accessed September 9, 2020.
8. "Management Minds: What Makes a Great Leader," DLANDROID24 website, August 25, 2002, https://dlandroid24.com/management-minds-what-makes-a-great-leader/, accessed September 9, 2020.

# Chapter 8: Experience

1. Matt Slater, "Olympics Cycling: Marginal Gains Underpin Team GB," BBC Sport website, August 8, 2012, https://www.bbc.co.uk/sport/olympics/19174302, accessed September 9, 2020.

2. Brian Merchant, *The One Device: The Secret History of the iPhone,* Chapter 9 (New York: Penguin Random House, 2017).
3. David Pierce and Lauren Goode, "The Wired Guide to the iPhone," *Wired,* July 12, 2010, https://www.wired.com/story/guide-iphone/, accessed September 9, 2020.
4. John Maeda, *How to Speak Machine: Computational Thinking for the Rest of Us* (New York: Penguin Random House, 2019).
5. Martin De Saulles, "Building a Virtuous Circle of Data-driven Innovation," CIO website, November 6, 2018, https://www.cio.com/article/3317524/building-a-virtuous-circle-of-data-driven-innovation.html, accessed September 9, 2020.
6. Oliver Lindberg, "UX Evolutions: How User Experience Drives Design & UI at Netflix," Adobe website, XD Ideas, April 12, 2019, https://xd.adobe.com/ideas/perspectives/interviews/interview-with-netflix-user-experience-drives-design-ui/, accessed September 9, 2020.
7. "Amsterdam's Robot Printed Footbridge Welds Steelwork with State-of-the-Art Technology," Arup website, https://www.arup.com/projects/mx3d-bridge, accessed September 9, 2020; Vanessa Liwanag, "World's First 3D-Printed Metal Bridge," ArchiExpo (May 6, 2020), http://emag.archiexpo.com/worlds-first-3d-printed-metal-bridge/, accessed September 9, 2020.

## Chapter 9: Engineering

1. C.K. Prahalad and Gary Hamel, "The Core Competence of the Corporation," *Harvard Business Review* (May-June, 1990), https://hbr.org/1990/05/the-core-competence-of-the-corporation, accessed September 9, 2020.
2. Mike Sutcliff, Raghav Narsalay, and Aarohi Sen, "The Two Big Reasons That Digital Transformations Fail," *Harvard Business Review* (October 18, 2019), https://hbr.org/2019/10/the-two-big-reasons-that-digital-transformations-fail, accessed September 9, 2020.
3. "Gartner Forecasts Worldwide Public Cloud Revenue to Grow 17% in 2020," Gartner website, November 13, 2019, https://www.gartner.com/en/newsroom/press-releases/2019-11-13-gartner-forecasts-worldwide-public-cloud-revenue-to-grow-17-percent-in-2020, accessed September 9, 2020.
4. Hope Reese, "Software Tests Are Essential in Improving Quality, But Most Developers Aren't Automating Them," TechRepublic website, June 18, 2020, https://www.techrepublic.com/article/software-tests-are-essential-in-improving-quality-but-most-developers-arent-automating-them/, accessed September 9, 2020.

5. "Software Developers," Bureau of Labor Statistics, US Department of Labor, *Occupational Outlook Handbook,* https://www.bls.gov/ooh/computer-and-information-technology/software-developers.htm#tab-6, accessed September 9, 2020.

# Chapter 10: Data

1. Rick Porter, "TV Long View: No Hits, No Problem – Cancel Rate for Rookie Shows Could Hit 10-Year Low," *Hollywood Reporter,* May 18, 2019, https://www.hollywoodreporter.com/live-feed/cancel-rate-rookie-shows-hits-10-year-low-2018-19-1211843, accessed September 9, 2020.
2. David Carr, "Giving Viewers What They Want," *New York Times,* February 24, 2013, https://www.nytimes.com/2013/02/25/business/media/for-house-of-cards-using-big-data-to-guarantee-its-popularity.html, accessed September 9, 2020.
3. Russell Walker, *From Big Data to Big Profits: Success with Data and Analytics* (New York: Oxford University Press, 2015).
4. Roberto Baldwin, "Netflix Gambles on Big Data to Become the HBO of Streaming," *Wired,* November 29, 2012, https://www.wired.com/2012/11/netflix-data-gamble/, accessed September 9, 2020.
5. Lucas Shaw, "Netflix Made More Films Than Any Other Studio. Now It Wants an Oscar," *Anchorage Daily News,* December 31, 2019, https://www.adn.com/arts/film-tv/2020/01/01/netflix-made-more-films-than-any-other-studio-now-it-wants-an-oscar/, accessed September 9, 2020.
6. Julia Alexander, "Netflix Is Straight Up Flexing at This Point," The Verge website, June 24, 2020, https://www.theverge.com/2020/6/24/21301959/netflix-july-2020-orginals-licensed-tv-movies-competitors, accessed September 9, 2020.
7. Carlos A. Gomez-Uribe and Neil Hunt, "The Netflix Recommender System: Algorithms, Business Value, and Innovation," *Association for Computing Machinery Transactions on Management Information Systems,* vol. 6, no. 4, Article 13, December 2015, https://dl.acm.org/doi/pdf/10.1145/2843948, accessed September 9, 2020.
8. Dave McCrory, "Data Gravity – in the Clouds," Datagravitas website, December 7, 2010, https://datagravitas.com/2010/12/07/data-gravity-in-the-clouds/, accessed September 9, 2020.
9. "Data Engineering, Preparation, and Labeling for AI 2019," Cognilytica website, March 6, 2019, https://www.cognilytica.com/2019/03/06/report-data-engineering-preparation-and-labeling-for-ai-2019/, accessed September 9, 2020.

10. S. A. Applin, "Everyone's Talking About Ethics in AI: Here's What They're Missing," *Fast Company,* June 14, 2019, https://www.fastcompany.com/90356295/the-rush-toward-ethical-ai-is-leaving-many-of-us-behind, accessed September 9, 2020.

## Chapter 11: Leading a Gryphon Organization

1. Barry Libert, Megan Beck, and Yoram (Jerry) Wind, *The Network Imperative: How to Survive and Grow in the Age of Digital* (Boston: Harvard Business Review Press, 2016) p. 191.
2. Shawn Tully, "Southwest Bets Big on Business Travelers," *Fortune,* September 23, 2015, https://fortune.com/2015/09/23/southwest-airlines-business-travel/, accessed September 11, 2020.
3. Jeff Bezos, Letter to Shareholders, April 11, 2019, Amazon website, https://blog.aboutamazon.com/company-news/2018-letter-to-shareholders, accessed September 11, 2020.

## Chapter 13: What Transformation Journeys Actually Look Like

1. Barry Libert, Megan Beck, and Yoram (Jerry) Wind, (2016). "To Go Digital, Leaders Have to Change Some Core Beliefs," Harvard Business Review website, June 1, 2016, https://hbr.org/2016/06/to-go-digital-leaders-have-to-change-some-core-beliefs#:~:text=Despite%20a%20great%20deal%20of,companies%20is%20this%3A%20not%20much.&text=Real%20digital%20transformation%20requires%20transformation,the%20leadership%20team's%20core%20beliefs, accessed September 11, 2020.
2. Sabrina McPherson, "Consumer Products: Unlocking Value from D2C Models," Publicis Sapient website, https://www.publicissapient.com/insights/unlocking-value-for-dtc, accessed September 11, 2020.
3. Thales S. Teixeira, *Unlocking the Customer Value Chain* (New York: Ballantine Books, 2019).
4. Rockwell Anyoha, "The History of Artificial Intelligence," Harvard University website, August 28, 2017, http://sitn.hms.harvard.edu/flash/2017/history-artificial-intelligence/, accessed September 11, 2020.

# Chapter 14: The Beginning

1. Glynn Davis, "Covid-19: Online Grocery Sales Nearly Doubled in Lockdown," Essential Retail website, June 23, 2020, https://www.essentialretail.com/news/covid19-online-grocery-double/, accessed September 11, 2020.
2. Leila Abboud, "L'Oréal Glimpses Its Digital Future Amid Pandemic," *Financial Times,* June 15, 2020, https://www.ft.com/content/ab917d5d-e601-44ba-9a2c-53dbb2146dc7, accessed September 11, 2020.

# Acknowledgments

A book such as *Digital Business Transformation: How Established Companies Sustain Competitive Advantage from Now to Next* is only made possible by the contribution of many hands and even more minds.

In writing it, I have been reminded just how ideas around business best practice and management theory circulate, iterate, expand, and, I hope, improve. For the thoughts, experiences, conversations, and connections that permeate this book, my first acknowledgments go to all of those people who, even unknowingly, have contributed. I am grateful to our clients and colleagues past and present, and to the thinkers and writers whose work has educated and inspired me.

Digital business transformation is always the culmination of the work of teams across organizations. It is not something you can do *to* companies or *for* companies, but *with* companies. Thank you to our clients for allowing us to partner with you on your transformation journey.

The book would not have happened without Lucy Devassy, who has championed, corralled, and contributed to the project from its inception through to completion, and Craig Smith, whose editorial craft has proved invaluable to its pitch and structure. They both have my enduring gratitude.

Publicis Sapient has been my incubator and sounding board. Without the people that have made it what it is over its 30-year history, the writing of this book would not have been possible. Publicis Groupe widened the opportunities for Publicis Sapient to make a difference, to operate, and to create greater impact, at the highest levels of business. I'm grateful to Maurice Lévy and Arthur Sadoun for that, and for the support that enabled the writing of this book.

My thanks go to our client leaders, thought leaders, and operational leaders across Publicis Groupe and Publicis Sapient who have been part of my journey and, in turn, the creation of this book. The list of people to recognize is long, but my gratitude to each of them is not diminished by that:

Abhishek Bhattacharya, Abhishek Rai, Adrian Sayliss, Adrienne Graham, Agathe Bousquet, AJ Dalal, Alan Clisch, Albert Fins, Alex Weishaupl, Alexandra von Plato, Alison Frees, Allison Bistrong, Alona Pugacova, Alyse Schwartz, Alyssa Altman, Amar Ellareddy, Amy Betty, Amy Hadfield, Anandha Ponnampalam, Andrea Pedrazzini,

Andrew Bruce, Andrew Lam-Po-Tang, Andrew Neustadter, Andrew Swinand, Andrew Wood, Andy Brawer, Andy Halliwell, Anil Garapati, Anita McGorty, Anjali Sinha, Ankaj Gupta, Ann Eckert, Anne Phelan, Anne-Gabrielle Heilbronner, Annette King, Anshu Prabhakar, Anshul Acharya, Antonio Newsom, Anubha Anubha, Anuja Ketan, Ariel Marciano, Arpit Jain, Ash Prashar, Ash Santimano De Souza, Ashley Snow, Ashutosh Joshi, Atul Mehta, Barbara Chai, Bassel Kakish, Ben Hwang, Bhumika Sharma, Bob Kasunic, Bob Van Beber, Boris Stojanovic, Brent Poer, Brian Clarey, Briana Lion, Bryan Kennedy, Caitlin Evans, Carina Moncivais, Carla Serrano, Caroline Calvet Hurst, Casey Craig, Cassandra Kelsall, César Croze, Chandan Banerjee, Charles Georges-Picot, Chirag Shah, Chloe Renaudin, Chris Loeffler, Chris Herzberger, Christian Waitzinger, Chris Hawkes, Cian Ó Braonáin, Dan Eagles, Dan Roche, Danielle Freymeyer, Danielle Gonzales, Danielle Meier, Dante Skidmore, Darach Ó Braonáin, Dave Murphy, Dave Penski, David Bernstein, David K. Donovan, David Gompel, David Taylor, David Whitehouse, Debleena Paul, Deepak Arora, Deepali Nayar, Delphine Stricker, Denise Antinori, Dennis DeYonker, Diana Littman, Dixit Patel, Doug Klesel, Eddie Gleeson, Edirin Onojaife, Eiko Kawano, Elizabeth Papasakelariou, Emma Scales, Emmanuel André, Erik Gottesman, Ernest Quarles, Erwan Moysan, Farnaz Haghseta, Fatima Alam, Fran Pessagno, Fran Sorrentino, Frank-Peter Lortz, Gemma Gordon-Gibson, Geraldine White, Gerry Boyle, GK Mishra, Guy Elliott, Haley Hackendale, Halley Marsh, Hans Scheidereit, Heather MacLeod, Helen Lin, Hilding Anderson, Hillary Klein, Ian Wharton, Iggy Harris, Isabella Carra, Isabelle Gélinet Vidal, Jagdish Ghanshani, James Kessler, James Whitaker, Jarek Ziebinski, Jason English, Jason Geddis, Jaspreet Singh, Javier Fernandez, Jean-Guy Saulou, Jean-Michel Etienne, Jean-Paul Brunier, Jem Ripley, Jennifer Burke, Jennifer Lee, Jennifer Steele, Jitender Batra, Jodi Robinson, Joe Tabita, Joe Weingartner, John Riley, John Sheehy, John Weston, Jon Panella, Jonathan Sharp, Julian Skelly, Julie Dickard, Justin Billingsley, Justin Plumridge, Kamal Karwal, Kamalesh Loganathan, Kameshwari Rao, Karin Giefer, Karishma Gupta, Karl Hall, Kate Woodward, Katie Murphy, Kendra King, Kim Nuzum, Kim Toomer, Kirk Friedenberger, Kristen Groh, Kristen Signore Brawer, Kristina Palmer Shedd, Lauren Goodge, Laurie Jadick, Lawrence Pearson, Lindsay Lichtenberg, Lisa Mahoney, Lise Malbernard, Liz Taylor, Lizzie Dewhurst, Loren Thomas, Loris Nold, Lou-Ann Paton, Magali Bergeroux, Maggie Lonergan, Magnus Fitchett, Manas Saha, Mandy Manning, Manu

Vaish, Mari-Ann Mortensen, Mark Berler, Mark Redwood, Mark Smith, Mark Watkins, Martin Davy, Masud Haq, Matt Drury, Matt Hopgood, Matt Locsin, Maulshree Singh, Maureen Piazza, Max Kirby, Michael Cohen, Michael Rebelo, Michael Wood, Michelle Kelly, Miki Brown, Milind Godbole, Ming Tsai, Mohammad Wasim, Monish Singhal, Mudit Kapur, Mumukshu Mohanty, Myla Young, Nader Nakib, Nadia Hussain, Nadira Kalliecharan, Nancy Rowe, Naomi Harlley, Naomi Tracey, Natasha Dagorn, Nathalie Le Bos, Naveen Soni, Nayan Kar, Neha Pathak, Nelson Pereira, Neville Bagot, Nick Colucci, Nick Ryan, Nick Shay, Nicolas Boin Principato, Niko (Nicholas) Papadakos, Nicole Hayes, Nidhi Chaturvedi, Noopur Shukla, Olivier Abtan, Olivier Goethals, Owen LaFave, Patrick Leclercq, Patty Sachs, Paul Bevan, Paul Dootson, Paul Gibson, Paul Mareski, Pawan Tayla, Peter Ekdahl, Peter Groves, Peter Szczerba, Phil Phelan, Philip Beil, Pinak Vedalankar, Piyush Jain, Prashant Singhal, Preeti Ravat, Priya Bajoria, Punit Mishra, Quinnton Harris, Rachel Hubel, Raj Chakraborty, Raj Shah, Raja Raman, Raja Trad, Raju Patel, Rakesh Ravuri, Ram Padmanabha, Raminder Bedi, Randall Orbon, Ravee Kurian, Ravi Evani, Ravi Narla, Ray Velez, Rebecca Werres, Reehan Sheikh, Renetta McCann, Ric Elert, Rishad Tobaccowala, Rishi Bhatnagar, Roberto Leonelli, Roma Sachdev, Ronald Shamah, Ronnie Dickerson Stewart, Ros King, Ruth Bayley, Ruth Smyth, Ryan Walsh, Sabrina McPherson, Sameer Bajaj, Sanjay Menon, Sara Lerner, Sarah Adam Gedge, Sarah Hoffman, Scott Clarke, Scott Criddle, Scott Petry, Sean McCarthy, Sean O'Donnell, Sean Peters, Sebastian Jandrey, Sharon Kamra, Shefali Garg, Sheldon Monteiro, Shikha Bajaj, Shireen Alam, Shiva Bharadwaj, Simon James, Sonali Fenner, Sooho Choi, Sophie Ghiggino, Srinivas Devulapalli, Sriram Appa Kunnathur, Stephane Dorel, Stephane Estryn, Stephen Aitken, Stephen Farquhar, Stephen Maltzman, Steve Birnbaum, Steve Bonnell, Steve King, Steven Metzmacher, Subbu Turimella, Sucharita Venkatesh, Sudeepto Mukherjee, Sudharsan Rangarajan, Sudip Mazumder, Sue Rockoff, Sunil Dodhia, Suse Menne, Symon Hammacott, Tanja Tuck, Teresa Barreira, Thibault Hennion, Thierry Elmalem, Thierry Quesnel, Thomas Bailey, Thomas Elkan Boisen, Tilak Doddapaneni, Tim Fathers, Tim Jones, Tim Lawless, Todd Cherkasky, Todd Meckenstock, Tom Budrewicz, Tony Tarle, Torben Pheiffer, Tracy Reilly, Trine Kane, Tulika Sanghi, Veronique Weill, Vicki Zoll, Vieshaka Dutta, Vini Nair, Vishnu Indugula, Vivek Puri, Wayne Townsend, Wendy Johansson, Will Fetchko, Yogita Sood, Zachary Paradis, and Zarul Shekhar.

I'd like to thank Sapient's founders Jerry Greenberg and Stuart Moore for their friendship and for creating a company so committed in purpose to making a positive difference in the world and grounded in core values. In 30 years of Sapient history, inevitably some close colleagues and leaders have moved on. Our paths may have diverged, but they are nonetheless an important part of my journey.

Thanks to Alan Herrick, Alan Wexler, Bill Kanarick, Chip Register, Chris Davey, Christian Oversohl, Clement Mok, Dan Barnicle, Donald Chesnut, Frank Schettino, Gaston Legorburu, Ian Cheewah, Ingo (Wolf Ingomar) Faecks, Joe LaSala, Joe Tibbets, John Maeda, Laurie Maclaren, Mike Reid, Peter Ford, Preston Bradford, Rajdeep Endow, Seth Bartlett, Sheeroy Desai, and Shubradeep Guha.

In any attempt to compile a list of individuals that have been a part of this project, some names will surely have been left out. To those people, I'd also like to express my gratitude.

# Index

## D

## W



## Y



## Z